UNLEASH YOURSELF

CLAIRE MACGILLIVRAY

To Jemma
What makes your heart
sing.

love from Claire MacGillivray ♡ Nov 2020

MINDSET MUM MEDIA

First published by Mindset Mum Media 2020

Copyright © Claire MacGillivray 2020

Written by Claire MacGillivray

Cover design and formatting by Helen Poole

To find out more about The Mindset Mum please visit www.themindsetmum.com or find her on Facebook at @themindsetmum.

ISBN 978-1-8382039-0-0

Dedicated to Aiden, Freya and Connor, who make my heart sing every day.

CONTENTS

INTRODUCTION

Change is horrible when you are not expecting it. It can unsettle and displace you in a heartbeat all without a whisper of a warning. This happened to me in August 2013. I was having a really 'normal' day; I had a friend round and we were just setting the picnic table in my garden with jugs of juice and sandwiches for the children when the phone rang. I don't normally answer it (I am the queen of the 'screen'!), but I looked at the phone and it was my partner Trev calling. Normally I would 'screen' his ass, especially at lunchtime, I don't want to hear about his work drivel while he chomps down on a sausage roll on the other end of the phone and I am trying to bribe our children to eat their crusts, but I felt compelled to answer it. Only it wasn't Trev, it was a woman on the end of the phone calling me by my name...

This was the moment that change came along and punched me right in the boob, that heart-stopping second that people talk about when telling you about momentous events in their lives. The woman was from the Kent Air Ambulance and told me that Trev was on his way to London's Kings College hospital and that I needed to get there as soon as possible, he had been involved in an accident at work and had suffered a brain injury. It was panic stations all around for me, what was I going to do with the kids? Where was Kings College hospital? How was I going to get there? What was I going to find when I got there? Not once did I think about the impact it was going to have on everything else outside of these few panic-stricken questions. This event changed everything about our life and very little would ever return to how we once knew it.

This was when I began to emerge from my cocoon.

Before Trev's accident I was just bouncing along with no real plan for life, just living day to day and having the time of my life, my two children (at the time) were the centre of everything I did and I had a great circle of friends around me to spend my endless days as a stay at home mum. I was not what you may consider as the planning ambitious type of woman. I was happy with my life as it was. I did not go seeking opportunities or embrace change in my life. I was afraid of what might be different and that made me uncomfortable.

Trev was in the hospital for three weeks, he had to learn to walk again and I had to do everything for him. I became a full-time carer overnight. With two children under four, this came with many challenges but the biggest change for us was Trev not going out to work every day. I was so used to him being gone every day that having him home was a real imposition never mind that he wasn't out making money to support us. I had to get used to him being around and looking after him. Living with a brain injury under your roof is not black and white and comes in all sorts of shapes and sizes. When Trev came home from the hospital he brought with him his invisible friends 'confusion' and 'rage' and I did not welcome their intrusion on my life. We fumbled through our first year of rehabilitation at home, getting things wrong more than we got things right. I am pretty sure we were in a constant battle with each other and I had permanently puffy eyes from the tears but somehow we made it through. It took 5 years to get Trev back to work but during that time I discovered ME and for this, I am truly grateful. They say things happen for a reason and every cloud has a silver lining and all that cheesy shit, but it is true. Every moment in our lives is happening to us for a reason and our job is to flow with it and embrace each moment with love.

I didn't have an epiphany one morning and as much as I want to tell those of you who are looking for that sign or that moment that signifies the emerging from your cocoon; that there is a moment when you feel the switch changing, there isn't. You perhaps won't even notice the change happen until you look back and perspective gives you the power to analyse a time differently allowing you to mark it as your turning point. Either way it does not matter, all that does matter is that you embrace what is happening to you in the moment and do not resist it.

I wanted to write a book that would resonate with people like me:

- **Busy**, I have three children and work full time and I have all the house crap to do.
- **Modern**, (note that I did not say fashionable! Think more, 'still shops in New Look and wears fake tan'). I read blogs, not magazines and I use social media to 'express' myself. I was a vegan until my mum fed me all the steak on my summer holiday, (totes not my fault for eating it), and I am still cool enough to wear a rucksack as my handbag. *That* kind of modern!
- **Woman**, well I don't need to prove myself

here, I have tits and a vagina the last time I checked and to top it off I gave birth to two children and the third was so big (eleven pounds kind of big) he needed to be removed via the sunroof.

I wanted to write a book that would actually get read, not just bought and put on the shelf, but is easy to read. Short enough that you can read it in a couple of nights and feel the accomplishment of finishing a book for once and not add it to the "I can't be arsed with this anymore" pile. But most of all I wanted it to feel like I was sitting with you having a chat over a coffee. I dislike books that tell me I should be doing this, that, and the next then fill me full of facts and information. I digest my advice best through stories and conversation and a relatable wee anecdote thrown in for good measure. I shall give you a wee heads up, although I shall not apologise for my use of language throughout the book. I wanted to keep the tone of the book true to my personality and as Billy Connolly said:

> *"Swearing is part of the poetry of working-class speech."*

If it's good enough for Billy, it's good enough for me, so fuck it!

My aim with the book is to help you feel better equipped to embrace change, perhaps even seek it out. The chapters are stand alone and I can confidently say you can pick up any chapter and take something away from it without needing to know the rest. Actually maybe one chapter you should all read is **What Makes Your Heart Sing?**, and **Society Says**, oh and *definitely* **It's Ok To Say No**, oh for fuck sake, just read the whole book from cover to cover. You have nothing to lose and everything to gain.

 Books do not change people; paragraphs do, sometimes even sentences.

— JOHN PIPER

What sentence will be the one that changes you?

TIME

> *Change will not come if we wait for some other person or some other time. We are the ones we've been waiting for. We are the change that we seek.*

— BARACK OBAMA

For most of us mere mortals living our human experience here on this glorious earth, time is a factor that plays a role, an incredibly significant role in our decision-making process, every day of our lives. Just for a moment, can you think of a memory where time was not a factor? Maybe a day completely to yourself? No one to be at home for? No children to pick up? No bedtime to consider? No emails to send? Nothing to do but just simply be in the moment? Can you recall a time where this has ever happened for you? This is not a trick question, there will be a time, even if it is a memory from your childhood that pops up, do not dismiss it, be aware of its place but acknowledge the lack of these available memories.

We tend to pride ourselves on being busy, maybe this comes from that place of fear and judgment of others who may consider us to be lazy or idle if not appearing busy enough. This is the impact society has on our way of thinking. As much as we believe our thinking is our own, it is the outcome of many different factors within our society which mould our mindsets, more on this later in the book.

It is so easy to get wrapped up in the mindset of not having enough time for this or for that. "I don't have time" is a universally accepted 'get out of jail free card' from having to do anything. "Oh, sorry I ran out of time to get back to you", "Oh sorry I can't do that favour you asked of me, I don't have time this week". "I don't have time" is the same as saying "I don't want to because I don't value the effort required from me for the return I am not sure I will receive". You may argue that you truly do not have the time, and you may genuinely believe this, but I would like to invite you to challenge this mindset as you read this book.

Would you ever say, "Oh shit I didn't have time to

feed the kids today" or "I didn't have time to get dressed this morning"? No of course not, because these are non-negotiables and programmed into your life for the beginning of your day. There are certain things we do which we do not have to think about having enough time for. With this in mind I would like to challenge your thinking around your own pre-set defaults each day. What do you do as part of your daily routine which is non-negotiable? For example, I do not like going to the gym, I have the time to I just don't want to. What are the non-negotiable activities for you? It is useful to know these and to identify them. This may seem silly to state but you would be surprised by the number of people who are not self-aware in this way.

The reality is, we all have time. We are all gifted with a fresh 24 hours every single day to live and breathe the air of this earth. Regardless of our race, gender, creed, or wealth, all humans have the currency of time in equal amounts. It is the one thing that is equal among all humans, time. How you spend it, well that is entirely up to you!

I want to show you something really simple, generic but effective in how we look at our time.

Meet Clarence, she is a busy working mum with three children and a husband. She gets up each morning at 6am and goes to bed at 10pm.

- Sleep 10pm to 6am = 8 hours
- Work 9am to 5pm = 8 hours
- Family time (cooking, eating, housework and watching TV) = 5 hours

These family and life commitments total 21 hours of her day, leaving Clarence 3 hours every day to herself!

3 hours a day is 21 hours a week to herself. What could she achieve in 21 hours per week? It is quite something when you see it in black and white. If you think of your time in this way and you can see on paper what you spend your time doing (or how much time you are wasting) your perspective may change. You now have the power of choice. This power enables you to make changes which you control.

There are many different variations of commitments you can add into this like the gym, caring for an elderly parent, etc. This is just an outline to engage your conscious thought.

Try writing this out for yourself. Without overthinking it, take an average day in the life of you, and note down how you break up your 24 hours.

 Time is free, but it is priceless. You can not own

it, but you can use it. You can not keep it, but you can spend it. Once you have lost it, you can never get it.

— HARVEY MACKAY

Prioritise the things that make your heart sing and you will find it easy to slot them into your day. I have listed ten different time-saving ideas for you to try for yourself. If you have any of your own which are unique and 'out of the box' thinking please feel free to share them with me on my social media. See the back of the book for links.

1. Stop watching TV.

Several years ago when I started my very first business I had convinced myself that I was an entrepreneur in the making and the fact I had two small children at home (at the time) would not stop me from running a home-based business. Only where was I going to find the time to run this business while I had kids at my feet and a partner that I was caring for? I decided to give up my evening soaps on TV. In this very moment I gained an extra two hours every day! 14 hours a week I was going to be a millionaire in no time at all! Although that wasn't quite how it worked out financially, I was a millionaire in the sense of time, as I now had an abundance of it each evening and had gained the feeling of self-fulfilment from doing something that made my heart sing. On the rare occasion I happen to catch five minutes of one of the soaps I used to watch, NOTHING HAS CHANGED, so and so is still cheating on his wife, someone else is still doing dodgy deals from the local garage and the couple who split up when I last watched it are now back together after divorcing each other. I apologise if you are a die-hard fan and love to fill your evenings watching soaps just please do not say you do not have time for something new or to engage in a growth activity when you consume so many hours watching trashy TV.

2. Stop scrolling social media.

This is a biggie! Studies have shown that on average we use social media for two hours a day. That is an insane amount of time to be staring at a screen mindlessly scrolling other people's lives. Seriously what is wrong with us?

Let me get one thing clear first and for all. If you are on Facebook then at least make sure you are a member of my tribe at @TheMindsetMum where at least you can be assured that a snippet of your screen time will include insightful value and of course my delightful charm!

Undertaking a social media cull is a little unrealistic and quite frankly it is a little prehistoric to think like that, so let's find a trendy way to solve our obsessive issue of peeping on each other (online of course, not accusing anyone of being a curtain twitcher). We can still hold onto our love of scrolling through each-others perfectly imperfect lives on social media, but set a timer so we can limit the stalking to a pre-decided time. I love a timer. They rule my life for me so I can be free to allow my mind to wander and be the creative machine that it is. Most people now have smartphones and I am fairly sure all smartphones have a timer facility on them. Take a look at your phone and familiarise yourself with where your timer app is. Now that you have located the timer, use the damn thing. Set a limit on how much time you are happy to freely scroll away, whether it's five mins or five hours (because well let's be honest, it's the weekend and you deserve it!). I also like to set boundaries for my social media time and as a rule I do not use it before 9 am on a weekday and I do not lie in bed before I fall asleep endlessly scrolling. Not only will this suggestion free up valuable time but also improve your wellbeing.

Spending less time on social media is a great thing for humanity!

3. Turn off notifications.

Damn the red dot which tries to rule our life! Do you ever look at your home screen and see a red dot screaming at you for attention? Girl, these are the group chat messages you have not read yet and I am not even talking about your unread emails. Go into the settings on your device and TURN OFF NOTIFICATIONS. Another little trick I learned was to move the worst offending apps to a different screen on my phone, anywhere but the home screen!

My worst offender for distractions is the group chat or the GC as I call it! The GC is the black hole of time. I love my girlfriends dearly and I would be lost without our GC, but I have officially lost count of the times I have put the kids to bed, read them a story, done the tickle backs and head rubs, then return to my evening only to find in that tiny capture of time, the GC has come to life and I now have 111 messages waiting for me. This shit stresses me out! I have to hide the app in my phone so I can't find it so easily.

Start getting some control back of your time and turn your notifications off so you are not being controlled by the red dot! Or at the very least, put your phone on silent during times when you are not designating screen time so that you can make the most of your time. Do not disturb is a good one for those of you who panic that someone won't be able to reach you if there is an emergency and your phone is on silent. Do not disturb allows you to customise who can call you without the worry of missing anything urgent.

Remember you are in control, do not let your life be controlled by the tiny red dot!

4. Get up earlier.

I bet you were wondering how long it would take me to mention this seemingly obvious suggestion to time management but in reality, it really does not need to be a painful suggestion in order to invoke change. An extra 15 minutes on your day is invaluable to you awake, not asleep. What could you do with this extra time? The magic here is to actually embrace the time, not to just enjoy having your eyes open lying in bed having an extra 15 mins to check your WhatsApp or dare I say it, SOCIAL MEDIA!

Get up. Drink a hot coffee. Meditate with your kids. Meditate alone. Dance. Prepare a healthy breakfast. Enjoy a longer shower. Read some of your book.

Write some of your book. Journal. Visualize. Connect. Be present and make the extra time count.

Fifteen minutes are doable and once you are embracing the time, start to stretch it out 20 minutes, then try half an hour. Imagine having an extra hour before your day would normally start! What could you achieve in this time? Head over to the Facebook community @TheMindsetMum and share your suggestions on how to be more productive with your time.

The gift of time is so precious and when you get into the habit of consciously creating more time for yourself you begin to live a more balanced life, and life becomes so much easier.

5. Meditate.

> *If you have time to breathe, you have time to meditate. You breathe when you walk. You breathe when you stand. You breathe when you lie down.*

— AJAHN AMARO

Now take a moment and think about what this means for you. Do you read those words and shrug them off or do you see the opportunity behind them? Herein lies your current mindset.

You may very well be saying to yourself right now that you are looking to find ways to make time in order to meditate in the first place. Let me share some 'no BS' wisdom with you. You do have the time already you are just not placing enough importance on what it can do for you. Take ten minutes tonight and listen to a guided meditation at bedtime as you drift off to sleep. You can download one of mine from my website (links at the back of the book) or find one on YouTube or on any of the multiple meditation apps you can access from your app store. There are no excuses, stop telling yourself there are.

Meditation in the morning for me is where the magic lies. Taking time out and severing the cord to the outside world; focusing my attention towards my heart and soul. Silence the outside world to hear the whispers of the Universe. To move your thinking from your head to your heart will enable you to be more streamlined and productive on the other side of your meditation thus saving you time. A regular practice of meditation will help you to focus on what is of importance to you by being spiritually guided.

6. Start saying NO!

Saying no to people can be hard especially when it's someone you love and they are asking something of you. But know this, you are the keeper of your time, it is yours to spend, share, and save however you see fit; saying no to something that does not make your heart sing is O.K. You have permission to say no to whatever does not make your heart sing.

If you start paying attention to how many offers come your way in a week that require you to take time from something else, it may surprise you how easy it is to have time slip through your fingers. Being proactive in how you spend your time will benefit you and also the person requesting it from you, as you are freeing the flow of energy for them to find someone who is a better fit for what they require.

It is not selfish to say no. It is self-fulfilling. Start to do it more often. Do more of what makes your heart sing and you will find yourself feeling happier from within and living in alignment with who you are.

7. Delegate tasks.

Sounds a bit corporate doesn't it! Not intentional I promise. I'm talking about delegating tasks around the home or chores if you will, although I dislike that word, it feels energetically heavy when I say it, a task feels lighter and more empowering like something good will happen as a result!

Get everyone involved, this is not parenting advice, just common sense. I will respectfully decline to answer any question relating to how to raise kids, however I have one opinion which is related to this tip which I simply cannot hold back! I do not believe in paying a child to do something that is a simple 'about the house' job. I do not get paid to tidy my room, so my kids do not. I definitely do not get paid to do the dishes so my kids sure as hell are not, the reason being that I do not want to create a negative money mindset. Some things in life we do because it makes our life more comfortable not because it makes us money. I do not judge others for their choice of encouragement and bribery, if I am totally honest here, I once cut the arm off my daughter's teddy after an ill-worded deal I made with her. She refused to stop doing what I asked her to, so Fifi got the snip. I must say that the satisfaction in knowing I would never be mistaken for the mum who goes back on her word was a memorable thrill and in the same breath I recoiled in my misguided authority and had to make a new deal with my four-year-old as I stood holding an armless Fifi. "Mummy would sew the arm back on if she helped mummy to do the thing she refused to do in the first place". So, I guess the only one who walked away with their dignity intact on this occasion was my darling four-year-old Freya!

By sharing the load of household tasks you are freeing up more time for yourself later in the day. It really need not be devastating for all to be involved, many hands make light work! I do not want to single out the reader who may not have children yet or indeed never intend to have any, with this delegation task in mind, could you afford a cleaner to come in and share the load with you? Could you offer a friend's teenage child a regular weekend job by cleaning your home or doing some odd jobs around the garden?

Do not try to be a hero and do all the work yourself then feel undervalued by the family for not appreciating your hard work. This has been a tough pill for me to swallow. I do not like asking for help. I like to do everything myself, I get this weird sense of virtue when I have completed a challenging job alone like building flat-pack furniture. I really do not like other people helping me, I enjoy doing it myself. It makes my heart sing to silently put bits of wood together with an Allen key and some dowels! However, I do not like losing a fingernail to it because I did not want to give in and ask for help.

I like to be independent and it comes from my way of life as a child growing up on the farm. From the moment I could walk and talk, all I wanted was to own a pony. I was obsessed. My poor family must have been driven nuts with my constant talking about the four-legged beauties. Despite my constant asking, Dad was very firm in that I would not be getting a pony until I was ten years old. Bloody hell that was a long way away when I was eight! If I wasn't going to be getting a pony I had to find something to fill my time with, playing hide and seek with my younger sisters had exhausted itself after the umpteenth time being the counter and leaving them hiding for ages at a time while I went off to dream of dressage and beach gallops. Mum and Dad were very hands off when it came to finding fun on the farm, so it was entirely down to me to entertain myself; I used to have this old sofa in my tack room, now this tack room was a place that my bestie Bonnie and I had built in eager anticipation for the day the pony arrived, never mind that we were two years premature! I had found an old bridle in my Dad's workshop (from when there were working horses on the farm). I hung the bridle on the edge of the gate and tied a sofa cushion onto the gate with bailer twine to make it look like a saddle. Bonnie and I would play on that gate for hours. I was so besotted with horses that in everything I did I practiced owning my own. I even rode my bike like I was doing the rising trot on a horse. The people who saw me on my way to the shops must have had a lot to say about that poor MacGillivray girl riding her bike in such a strange way.

Doing things out of the learned behaviour to be independent does not win you medals! Learn to accept help and to get comfortable asking others for their help. In the end, I had to ask Bonnie to help me as I couldn't get the bailer twine around the gate and the mighty cushion with my little eight-year old arms on my own! People cannot read minds, so if you do not ask, you do not get!

Delegating tasks is such a fab way of saving time on the mundane jobs that do not make your heart sing and make way for more time to spend on the things that really set your soul alight.

8. Schedule time for what is important to you.

Please, if all you take away from this book is this small paragraph then I have achieved what I set out to do with this book. Do not fall victim to the black hole of time. For time is, in essence non-existent, it is merely our perception of time that we are beholden to. Telling yourself, your children, your partner, your friends, your family, that you do not have time to do XYZ is a slap across the face. We all have time, we just prioritise it differently. To tell your child that you don't have time to read a bedtime story is telling them you don't think reading a bedtime story is important enough to push back what you have to do that evening. You can get your chest all puffed out and start flapping your arms around at this statement, but it is true.

You may have heard of diary blocking, time blocking, etc. before. Scheduling in the non-negotiables each week/month is something you could get used to. Smartphones are wonderful devices and have lots of features available to us to enable us to set timers, reminders, alerts, anything you can possibly imagine to enable good timekeeping and scheduling. This could be as simple as blocking out 45 minutes every Wednesday to apply a face mask to improve your skin. If it is important to you, make it happen. Do not wait for the right time to fall into your lap, looking back on the last few years, can you honestly say that this approach has been successful for you? Time waits for no one.

An old friend of mine from many moons ago used to have a non-negotiable night in the week she called her beautifying night. Everyone knew about it and nobody messed with it. We all knew that regardless of what the temptation or party there was to attend, nothing was that tempting to push aside beautifying night. When I first met her I thought it was weird that she had such a rigid routine for her skincare because she already had such great skin so why was she making such a fuss about it! Well of course it was this commitment to herself that she had developed such gorgeous and enviable skin in the first place.

Whatever it is that you are currently banging the drum of not having enough time for, start prioritising it. You will soon start to see when the phrase "I don't have time" is actually being used as a polite way of saying, "I don't like your suggestion and it's really not that important to me". Why not challenge yourself NOT to say "I don't have time" for one week and list all the things that come up which you felt you were inclined to say it to and review it. Change your mindset on time.

9. Go to bed a little later.

As much as getting up earlier seems like an obvious option, albeit possibly reluctant for many! How about going to bed that little bit later in the evening. No, I am not talking hours later I am simply suggesting half an hour. That is time to read ten pages of a book, meditate, reply to your bestie's message from days ago or to write a list of gratitude about your day.

Be realistic about what you want this extra time for. If you just want time to sit in silence or to feel like the day has not owned you, then stealing time in this way for yourself is such a high vibe place to be. Your wellbeing will benefit greatly. Be mindful of not allowing the time to be swallowed up by scrolling social media or replying to work stuff, unless of course, this is what you want the extra time for in the first place!

10. Manifest it!

Yes, you can indeed manifest more time. You can manifest anything you desire if you do it in the right way. It is all energy and playful force. The more and more you say you do not have time, the more evidence of this being true you will see. Try flipping the phrase on its head. Feel grateful for the abundance of time you have, how you enjoy taking time out from each day to just be in the moment, embracing the beauty of life all around you, all the wonderful things you want to achieve when the time is right for it to happen. This vibration or feeling is a playful and easy energy to hold onto. The possibilities feel endless with this mindset. Think of it as beating the drum of what you desire. Esther Hicks very famously talks about how beating the drum of the things we wish not to see is only bringing those things closer and closer to us, as the Universe knows no difference between like and dislike, only to the vibration of the desire which we are focused upon.

When thinking about manifesting more time visualise and believe the imagination, allow yourself to think about the benefits of more time. What will it do for you? What will you do with it? How will it make you feel? Focus on the positive outcome.

One of my favourite stories to tell about manifesting time is about an evening I was out driving my son to his Taekwondo school and we were running a touch late. We were approaching a scrappy little lane en-route to the school and it is notorious for being full of potholes, crazy drivers, and very narrow passing places. Very rarely had I ever driven it and not met a single car along it. However this evening I was thinking about how lovely it would be to have a clear passage down this road and how my son would be so impressed when I got him to class on time, despite his worries he would be late. I held onto this energy as I was driving along the road, each corner I approached I was convinced that it would be clear and I would not have to step on the breaks, I would sail along with ease and grace and arrive with time to spare. I received exactly what I was asking for, a completely clear passage, not a single car was to be passed. Give it a go yourself. Anything is possible.

Time is so precious to us all. As the mind gets older,

time seems to pass faster. So slow down for a moment and adopt something from the ten tips you have just read. We can not change time, nor can we hold onto it. We can however make the most of every moment, so be present in the now.

The past can not be changed.

The future is unwritten.

The only moment ever in existence is right now. This very moment.

2

WHAT MAKES YOUR HEART SING?

 Be so busy doing what you love; that you have no time for bitterness or hate.

— KAREN SALMANSOHN

Making your heart sing is a conscious act of awareness, you may just have never noticed it before; I want to help you to tune your ears to the vibration of your soul. Your heart is the arrow in your spiritual compass; when you learn to live life in more balanced alignment, your heart becomes the beacon by which you are led.

What does it mean to make your heart sing? If you think about the words for a moment and imagine what this feeling may be to you. When I think of my heart singing I think of something that makes me genuinely happy, down to my heart happy. It's the simple things in life that are right in front of you, they are all around you if you choose to look for them. Getting into my bed after my bedsheets have been washed and dried on the washing line, the smell of outside but inside and all around me as I sleep, that kind of happiness cannot be bottled or reproduced, it just simply makes my heart sing.

For lots of people not knowing what your passion is or what simple pleasures in life you treasure when asked causes a deep feeling of stress and uncertainty. I spent the first 30 years of my life not being connected to this simplicity of thought. I knew what I enjoyed doing or what I thought was fun but associating the vibration of happiness and love to a simple joy in life was far beyond my cognitive thoughts. This is the difference between living life and living a balanced life. When you make the change in your mindset to consciously change what and how you think, your whole perspective becomes clearer. Kind of like when you finally discover the resolution slider on your phone after months of squinting at it in the daylight, then all of a sudden you can see it in full colour and you wonder how you managed for so long with such a dull screen. It changes what you look at. My comparisons are remarkable don't you think?

> *If you change the way you look at things, the things you look at change.*

— PROFESSOR MAX PLANCK

Sometimes when simple changes are offered to us, we begin to wish that we had thought of it ourselves; a feeling of regret can whip at our heels. Regret is a vibration to avoid, let go, and accept that you are learning something at this moment which will improve your life. You have received this 'gift' at the exact moment in time for you and has been planned all along. Be excited for the change which awaits you when you begin to act on these insights as this can mark the beginning of your turning point.

On reflection, my turning point seems more like a year rather than one 'ah-ha' moment. During this self-discovery period, I began to tune into my spiritual curiosity and started to figure a few things out about who I was and what was important to me; this is not a road with a single destination this will be a lifelong journey and as things change around you, you will be inspired to make changes to your mindset but it will feel right and easy to do so. Change, for most of us has some negative connotations to it and can ignite fear within us. Through this book I want to re-write the rules on this suggestion.

The first daily change I made was simple, I started to do something every day that made my heart sing. And you know what? This little shift in my mindset changed my life dramatically for the better. Have you ever heard the saying where focus goes energy flows? Making a deliberate effort every day to look for simple joys, to make your heart sing programmes your consciousness to seek out the good stuff in your day. Think about this in reverse, do you ever wake up and say to yourself "I feel like shit" or "I'm so tired"? Does your day ever surprise you and become the best day of your life? No of course it doesn't, why would it? You have already decided to look for the shit storm in your day, so guess what girl? You are going to have a shit day! If you tell me otherwise I shall call you out for talking shit! The Law of Attraction states that we manifest into life what we vibrate at our core, so with this in mind, take conscious control of what you tell yourself and how you interpret what you see and feel.

Make that decision today. Do not put it off until tomorrow. If you want to initiate positive change in your life, do it right now. The easiest thing to do in any given moment is to observe the space around you, what can you see which you can choose to see the joy in? Just take a few seconds to observe what you see and feel the joy within you, can you feel your heart singing?

Maybe positivity is not your natural outlook but that is not to say you cannot change the way you respond to observation and make positivity your default perspective. Remember you get to choose. Every response in life is a choice, YOUR CHOICE to make. So, choose wisely.

Are you thinking that maybe there is more to this heart singing lark than I cared to share in the beginning? I have a whole chapter to fill on it, so I need to find something to say about it! Seriously though, it is really simple, start your day by looking for something to find joy in, it can be anything from reading or running to dancing or helping a friend, the list is endless. When you can consciously take control of your happiness, your feeling of confidence and fulfilment will be so much more prominent. You have the beginnings of mindset mastery and your curiosity will drive you to explore more of your spirituality which will invite more balance into your life.

Your happiness is 100% within your control. Yes, other people can contribute to the scales tipping in either direction at any given moment in time, but just remember that ultimately you cast the deciding vote on what you allow yourself to focus on and what you don't. If something does not make your heart sing, make an empowered decision to say no, there is a whole chapter coming up on this controversial conversation around how to say no to people, so prepare to get pissed off with me as you may not find it an easy read!

Choosing to look for reasons to be happy or to find things that make your heart sing is taking a huge step towards energetic balance and it is available to you at every moment. Your perception is your power so be in full unapologetic control of how you perceive any moment. Choose to see and feel more positively and you are launching the rocket of desire for more of the same experience to come back to enjoy, the Universe is very generous like that. Do not wait for the good stuff to happen to you go out there and make it happen for yourself. You are the creator of your own destiny.

Making your heart sing is felt on a physical and emotional level it is not just empty words. You can feel it happening. It is like your heart warms up and is getting larger in your chest for the moments you feel it happen. Your face stretches into a large smile that you are not in control of and nobody can take it away from you.

It need not be a huge gesture that you are looking for and I promise you, when you start to look for the stuff that makes your heart sing you will begin to notice it all around you. For me, the small stuff is just as important as the big stuff like the sound of the bath running which my kids have run for me, the smell of my neighbour cutting the grass outside, the smell of freshly line-dried bed sheets, the taste of the first strawberry from my garden. Train your mind to look for the good stuff all around you and the more of it you will find. Savour the experiences and make a mental note of them, it is one of the fastest ways to vibrational alignment and taking a lead of your mindset. It is not about taking control of your mindset, rather consciously leading it along the path of love.

Bringing your children into this daily habit is a fabulous way to instigate emotional confidence and the belief that they can be in the driving seat of their happiness and awareness. Teaching your children is not always about the sit-down talk and explanation, it is in the 'walking the walk' and 'talking the talk' openly at home about daily challenges which you are working through. Mastering our mindset is a lifelong commitment it's not about waiting until you are thirty odd like I was, it is about teaching our children at a young age so it becomes so normal for them to be in tune with themselves like this.

When I think of the generation of children who are growing up in households who take this approach to vibrational balance and their mindset, it makes my heart sing at the limitless possibilities which will open up to them.

It is so simple to make your heart sing and a foundational element in defining balance. I think I may have said this at the end of every chapter in the book! It's really hard to choose which steps are more important than others! But I do have to say that making your heart sing is pretty high up there on the importance scale as it is the foundation that on which everything I coach is built upon - it's really easy to do and you get instant results from it.

3

SOCIETY SAYS

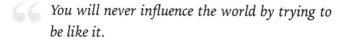 *You will never influence the world by trying to be like it.*

— UNKNOWN

Like the good old game *Simon Says*, the title suggests where I am taking you in this chapter.

As a child I always was a bit of a rebel; I did not like to be told what to do, when to do it and definitely not how to do it. If I was told not to do something I needed to know why or I was going to have to find out for myself one way or another. I distinctly recall my Dad telling me "never lick a frozen gate" much like we are told not to eat yellow snow, although there is no little limerick to go along with "do not lick a frozen gate". There is a distinct possibility that this is more a farm girl problem than a widely faced winter conundrum for children under the age of twelve. Picture the scene from the film Dumb and Dumber where Lloyd licks the frozen chairlift as he is approaching the exit slipway. Yes, yes, I did indeed lick a frozen cattle gate on my way to school one morning when I was probably far too old to admit to such a moronic act. In an instant, I realised why dad had warned me not to. However I was satisfied in my discovery that the sparkly, crystal formations on the silver gate glistening in the winter sunlight, were indeed the DEVIL in disguise and would haunt me for the rest of my life! Every time I lick an ice-lolly my body recalls the panic of being stuck to the gate and having to rip my tongue from the devilish trap.

I did not like to conform as a child and I am even more adamant in digging my heels in now. I do not feel like I fit into the society around me, it has taken me time to grow comfortable in my own skin and to find my place in the world I live in. Throughout this chapter, I want to help enable you to sever some of these ties that society has beholden upon you. Not to turn you into a rebel but to help you realise that we are all doing things in our day that we could admit do not make our heart sing yet we feel we must do them to appease someone or some feeling you have that you NEED to be doing it. I want to help free you to do more of the stuff that makes your heart sing.

In recent years I have become increasingly aware of the world around me and how much or often how little I know about it; I have an obsession to understand how my mindset has evolved, but more importantly, what has formed my views and perspective of the world I see in the first place. What have I heard, read, or watched which has moulded a particular view or belief? This mindset really does play a huge role in any aspect of your perception. Some people say perception is power, this in itself is arguably dependent upon your own personal perception. I prefer to see kindness and love as power.

The world around us is confused and depending upon where you look it can seem like an extremely negative place. There is a lot of hate, judgment, segregation, division, and fear which is fed to us through the press, global politics, social media, social circles, does this list even have an end? I have consciously decided to take a different perspective on the world by learning from my own mistakes and from those of others who have trusted me with their stories or in my selfish search to find someone else as hopeless as myself; clinging on to the idea that there is always someone suffering more hardship than me. I sometimes find myself sifting through books and online stories until I find a suitable anecdote to satisfy my thirst for superiority.

When something doesn't feel right to me I listen to my intuition and choose my own path. I do not allow others to make my decisions or try to shape my view of the world. But it is not easy to ignore the masses; humans by their very own genetics are evolved to mimic and follow other humans. It is too easy to fall into the trap of becoming moulded by society or to find yourself living a life that does not make your heart sing. Arguably I have become moulded, but I like to think by my own choosing, however this is open to debate!

You have the freedom to choose what you feel is good for you. Forget keeping up with the Joneses. Do you really want to become the statistic which is the basis of this understanding famously talked about by Jim Rohn; "You are the average of the five people you spend the most time with"? Now before you grab for the paper bag and begin hyperventilating, this does not mean you have to cleanse your circle today and begin sending breakup texts to life-long friends. But if you want to use me as a scapegoat to rid yourself of some dead wood in your circle, by all means, send that Dear John, and maybe while you are at it, send them a copy of this book with this chapter bookmarked, no other explanations needed!

Sometimes all it takes is reading the words in black and white to know that it is OK to stand out. It is OK to want to change and become a different person to who you were yesterday. It is OK to say no and do something different. Be the change you want to see in yourself. All change begins in the first footstep. You are on the right path by simply picking up this book in the first place, change is within all of us willing to cast aside society's blueprint for you. Be the butterfly that is waiting to emerge from your soul.

Think about how many advertising images you have seen in your lifetime. Not just the ones you see, but the ones your subconscious mind sees. Advertising is not to be taken lightly, this is a science, and people study for years to understand how the right colours, the specific sound, the duration of exposure, everything down to the time of day you are expected to view the message is calculated. Let alone the images and logos around your home which you are exposed to all the time. You only need to play a game of 'Logo' to begin to understand how advertising has had a dramatic effect on what you believe to be true about the world. What is remarkable about this is the sheer amount of subconscious programming we create about ourselves and our environment based on what we believe to be true or acceptable. The colours, the words, the fonts, the people, the accents, the clothing, the cars, the money, the food, the language the list is endless. These are all factors in creating what we think we know about ourselves and the world we live in, this is our belief system.

Let me run a test on you. When you read the following few words, what springs to mind?

JUST DO IT

Does it mean anything to you? Does your mind's eye create a picture for you?

Nike, the sporting goods giant, you know, the one with the big tick logo. For me, *Just Do It* is so familiar! If you have no clue what the reference means, no need to worry, I am not testing you on your big brand knowledge. What I want to highlight is the common use of words and images which create sub-conscious meanings to us.

Society has had its way with most of us, subliminally programming our minds to see and believe things whether they are in fact there or not. Now you may be wondering what on earth this has to do with your spiritual mindset, I have a train of thought so stay with me I am just getting to the juicy bit!

Arguably between the ages of seven and eleven, our

core beliefs about human behaviour are being developed in our brains and we create beliefs that will shape and mould our lives as we grow up and become young adults. Take a breath, do not panic, you are not currently 'breaking your children' if you were not aware of this before now. Now is the time to make the change.

The secret is to work on YOU first! There has never been a better time to become more aware of your own mindset than now. Children are mirror images of us, what they know, and how they behave is a direct reflection of us as parents and how we express our mindset and views of society. Becoming aware of this is so powerful. Your role in raising kind and well-adjusted young adults into our world is so important. Taking an actively conscious perspective on the conversations and explanations you have with your children at all ages is key to their wellbeing and ability to adjust within our changing society.

Nothing makes me smile more than when I hear one of my children repeat something I have imparted on them during one of my "my mum used to say this to me when I was a child" conversations. Do you ever do that when speaking to a child; think of them telling their children that you used to say this to them, and it has stayed with them throughout their life? There may be a possibility I have placed a huge amount of importance on the conversations I have with my children! It certainly sounds a lot like I think I have a great deal of wisdom to share. I really hope this does not come back to bite me in the ass at some point in the future! "But mum you said, that if I felt I had a point to make, despite what the adult is saying, make my voice heard, I may be a child, but I have the right to be heard". Oh God, I can hear it now, my poor child waiting to speak to the headteacher and then the voice of my parents "children should be seen and not heard". All I can do is hope for the best and send those children out into the world with a heart full of love and a head full of kindness, and all my fingers crossed!

I want you to feel empowered to become aware of your own ties to society. What do you do out of obligation for others? How do you feel about the things that are fashionable, not just clothing but TV shows, home style, the car you drive, where you live, where you holiday? It's all the things we do because it's what society makes us feel we should. Being aware of it is all you need for now. You may not feel that there is any negative effect on your mindset due to the pressure of society yet. That is fantastic if you feel like this. But for many of us, this 'permission to feel' is incredibly liberating.

You can bring balance to your mind by practicing mindfulness to help negate the overstimulating world outside your door. Taking a few moments to be present in your body, wherever you may be, fixate your attention onto an object or a feeling within your body. Mentally scan it up and down and absorb the colours you may observe, feelings, smells, sounds, or tastes. Bring your five senses to life and let them bring the object of your attention to life inside your mind's eye. You need not over-think this exercise, you simply want to let go of all thought beyond what you focus your attention on, should you feel yourself wandering and your mind will wander, just become aware of this and bring it back to the focus at hand. Mindfulness is really helpful for children to weave into their daily lives. It is such a helpful tool to learn to help bring the feeling of balance into any given moment.

Society dictates an awful lot about our lives, and we are all guilty of allowing it to happen. Even when you are aware that it is happening sometimes it is just so much easier to allow than to resist. Now for a moment, I am going to contradict myself. As a mindset coach, I spend a lot of time encouraging my audience to allow energy to flow. Allow, allow, allow never stop allowing that flow! But when it comes to matters outside our lives that are causing a direct effect on our physical body or our mind and we have identified that it does not FEEL good, we must take ownership of that and step away. This is true for even the toughest of realities, those relationships we really do not want to admit are poisonous to us, the career change you know you need to instigate. But change is where the magic begins.

You have the strength within you to make a positive change. You are stronger than you think.

4

MEDITATION IS THE MULTI-VITAMIN FOR YOUR SOUL

> *You do not need to be great to start, but you have to start to become great.*
>
> — ZIG ZIGLAR

In my humble opinion everyone should make time in their lives to experience the benefits of this magical medium on a daily basis or at the very minimum once a week. Please do not get wrapped up in the bullshit lies you want to tell yourself about not having the time to meditate regularly, did you not take anything away from Chapter One? Do you think you want to make a positive change in your life? But do you really expect to be able to do this without making a time commitment to yourself?

Full disclosure, I can feel the rising feeling of utter hypocrisy as the words are leaving my fingertips on the keyboard; I make it sound like I meditate every day, I am the first to hold my hands up and say it does not always happen every day for whatever excuses I have made up to myself, but let me tell you a little secret about this 'mindset mastery' journey we are upon, on the days that I don't meditate in the morning, I can feel it. I am less productive, I am more shouty at the kids, I am more stressed with life and the people that wind me up on the journey through my day! I can feel it in my brain fog, my thoughts are crowded and I am less focused on gratitude and utter love for my life. When I begin to feel this happening in my day, I stop dead in my tracks and go somewhere quiet to take a few meditative moments to myself.

On these days that I do not make time for meditation during my waking hours, I make damn sure I take moments at bedtime to sit in silence and detach myself from the buzz of the day. I let my thoughts fall to the wayside and I freefall into the multiverse, completely vacant of thought and feeling before I drift off to sleep.

We are all living super busy lives, some arguably busier than others, although this does not negate the of degree of busy you deem yourself to be.

Everything is relevant within our own circumstances. But there is never a good enough excuse to neglect your wellbeing. You can not drink from an empty cup. It is your responsibility to do the things that bring out the best in you and I hope that through reading this book you will decide on the things you want to incorporate into your life. Yes, I did say "you decide" but allow me to make one suggestion, make meditation a priority. If you do nothing else to make a positive change in your life forevermore but adopt a meditation practice that works for you, you will see SIGNIFICANT improvements in all areas of your life. It really is that powerful.

Meditation is something I have learned on my own personal journey through life on my spiritual quest to feel more balanced and aligned. It is a huge part of our family life. Before I became attuned to my growing spirituality, I had this view of what I thought meditation was and those who took part in such hippie activities. These crazies were, in my very naïve opinion mountain living, razor phobic, tie-dye wearing vegans. Such brutal honesty tells an awful lot about the mindset I used to have. Now let me share something ironic with you, I am now that hippie. I love using tie-dye and if you were to ever visit my home, there is an exceedingly high chance that you would spot a tie-dyed item hiding in plain sight P.S I hate shaving my legs!

The practicality of silence.

Meditation itself is the practice of oneness with yourself. Silencing your mind of thought and emotion; instead, focusing your attention inward towards your true self, your inner being, your soul, YOU. It takes a little practice to get to the point where your mind no longer wanders during meditation. Even my mind still wanders during my practice if I am particularly distracted, but over the years of practice, I have learned how to come back to the sound of silence. It does take practice and persistence, but this is not to say you will not benefit from meditation the very first time you do it, spending any length of time alone in silence is hugely beneficial. You build confidence in yourself the more you consistently meditate and of course the more you practice, the longer your meditation sessions can last which will ultimately grow the feeling of balance within you.

There are two different types of meditation, guided and solo. Guided is where you listen to the sound of someone's voice 'guiding' you along an imagery pathway; for you to free your mind of active thought.

Solo is where you have become experienced enough to sit in the silence of your own mind and be completely devoid of thought during the chosen length of time for your meditation with nothing but a bell timer to bring you back to reality.

Guided meditation is an absolute joy for everyone when they are first starting out. You simply hit play on the meditation of your choice and listen to the sound of the voice speaking. Attach your thoughts to their words and not on the multitude of tasks you have told yourself you need to complete. If you find your mind wandering first of all this is totally normal, your mind is not programmed to switch off from your daily life, we are programmed to be plugged in and turned on at any given moment! Recognise that your mind has wandered from the sound of your guiding voice and come back to the words. Let go of any anxiety about time or that you should be doing something else. You can download a guided meditation narrated by me from my website. I shall insist on you putting your book down right now to go and do that before you go any further.

Meditation is a deeply personal experience and not one size will fit all. Not everyone who downloads my meditation will enjoy my style, my Scottish accent, or the tone of my voice. Do not ever tell me this though, my ego has taken a big enough hit through revealing myself in this book to last me a lifetime! I implore you to keep this secret of rejection to yourself. On the other hand, if you do indeed enjoy listening to me, feel free to tell me! You can ping me an email or connect with me on social media, you will find the links at the back of the book. This sort of feedback is welcomed by my ego! Let it flow, flow, flow!

Experiment with different meditations and find out what works best for you. I am personally not a great fan of strong accents or music in the background of a guided-meditation. There are loads of different places you can look for free meditations. Your app store is a good starting place. I personally like Insight Timer but do your own due diligence and see what you like and what you don't like. There is nothing more annoying than sitting down to meditate and finding the voice so irritating that you can't focus on the freefall of thought because you are obsessing over the drilling sound of the voice you are listening to!

Solo meditation is the goal and consistent practice will help you get to this point where you are confident to sit in your own silence. I like to play some babbling brook sounds in the background or the sound of the rolling waves in the ocean with a timer on to bring me back to reality at the end of my meditation. It really enables me to free my mind and detach myself from the tentacles of life. It does take time to be able to free yourself of the self-sabotaging talk that wants to chatter away in the background or remind you that you have unticked tasks on your to-do list from last week. And before you know it you have spent five minutes down the rabbit hole of thought and you conclude that you have now wasted all that time fretting over it all that you may as well open your eyes and get on with the day and attempt meditation another time. Well, we all know what happens when we allow ourselves to quit! Recognise this thought and come back to your awareness of the gap between one and two. If you slowly count in your mind, 'the gap' is that moment in-between one and two. The gap is where you want your mind to hang-out. Try it now, wherever you are, just for a few moments, close your eyes and count slowly to ten. Savour the moments in-between each number. As you count higher up the numbers make the gap bigger stretch it in your mind and be aware of the gap it may feel awkward at first like a lull in conversation with a stranger but embrace this freedom of thought. Be in the moment within that gap. Put the book down and try it.

Did your mind wander in those moments?

Everyone I get talking to whether it is a client or a stranger in the supermarket queue will hear me banging on about the magical powers of meditation and the importance of a regular practice. It is not a question of "do you have time to meditate?" But a question of "do you have time NOT to?" Assuming you didn't skip chapter one and you are already putting some of the tips into practice to manifest more time in your day; you will already have created pockets of time in your day which you have rescued that you can devote to meditation.

One thing I must ensure is that you never give yourself guilt for skipping a meditation. If you miss it once it is not the end of the world, but you will notice the feeling of disconnect. Be aware of this and make a time sacrifice to sit for a few minutes to reconnect. No-one can make change happen for you, it is solely your responsibility.

Be generous with this new gift you have found and share it with your children. Please don't dismiss meditation with children, you will be surprised how quickly they can connect to the vibration of silence and feel calm and rejuvenation from just a few minutes of guided meditation. There are so many ways that meditation can easily slot into our busy modern lives. I am pretty confident that almost every home would have a way of playing a meditation in a child's bedroom at bedtime as they fall asleep. In place of an imagination igniting audiobook, play a relaxing meditation. Or you can learn to narrate your own meditation so instead of reading a story at bedtime for younger children, you guide them through the meditation with your voice, perhaps record it on a voice recording app which can be played through a Bluetooth speaker. The possibilities are endless with meditation.

5

FILL YOUR CUP

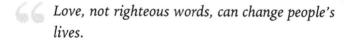 *Love, not righteous words, can change people's lives.*

— HAEMIN SUNIM

In this chapter I would like to give you a few things to consider when thinking of how to 'fill your cup'. It may seem really obvious to you, in fact a lot of the stuff I touch on in this book may seem really obvious to you BUT, are you actively putting any of this stuff into practice, enough to manifest actual positive change happening? More often than not it is the simple stuff that is written between the lines of life which lies there motionless and staring us in the face until someone taps you on the shoulder, in this case me, and points your attention towards something that may make your life a little bit more balanced.

When we fly, during the emergency demonstration at the beginning of the flight, (which you all pay your full attention to of course!), the flight attendants mention the air masks that will fall from the panel above should the need for oxygen arise. The cabin crew then go on to explain that you must put on your own mask before helping others. I must be honest I never really paid much attention to this piece of advice. I always thought that as a mother I would of course save my children first and find the nearest oxygen mask and give it to them before putting my own on. Now halt and note my error of judgment and naivety in this thought process. If I do not put my oxygen mask on BEFORE I help my children, the chances are I may end up unable to breathe or help my children at all as a result of my actions.

Consider the cup is a metaphor for your mindset. If you are feeling empty and run down, can you take anything of value from yourself? Can you think about being the source of inspiration and balance to another person? If you have allowed yourself to become over-run with stress and anxiety, are you performing a duty of care to yourself? This is a rhetorical question of course.

You must look after yourself first and foremost. Get it out of your head that it is selfish to do so. Filling your cup is the same as putting on your oxygen mask first.

Fill your cup with goodness for your soul to strengthen your mindset before you can expect to inspire those around you and impart wisdom. This is not intended to add another thing on the list of things to do in life. This is a mindset to adopt and to challenge yourself daily. Am I high vibration today? If not, why not? What can you do right now to make yourself feel better? This is simple stuff, little tweaks you can make to how you think or act. As insignificant as telling yourself you are awesome when you look in the mirror. All these small incremental efforts build on each other and form a kick-ass, unshakable feeling within you.

Take time out for you as a priority. Make it a non-negotiable daily/weekly/monthly appointment for yourself where you recognise you for all that you are and feed your soul with all the goodness that it deserves. This action is essential for your wellbeing. You simply cannot drink from an empty cup. Set a reminder on your phone to pop up as frequently as it will be effective; a reminder on my phone that pops up every day becomes unnoticed, I ignore it much like I do the holes in my socks, I see them but it doesn't spur me into action to do something about it. So put your reminders at times and places around your home or work that will invoke action not merely observation.

Try weaving it into your day among the other regular activities you do; like brushing your teeth and while you look in the mirror tell yourself you love you, tell yourself your goals and aspirations. When you are in the shower, run through a list of things you are grateful for. This stuff does not need to get in the way of your life, just weave it into the things you already do.

Find what works for you and what makes your heart sing. For me, I make a conscious daily effort to read, not my social feed, but a real-life book, with paper pages I can touch and feel between my fingers, I would be lying if told you I read ten pages every day, but I pick it up every day and immerse myself in it for as long as I can as often as I can. Some days this may be a one-hour read-a-thon and others it may be just five minutes before someone starts fighting or yelling "muu-um" from the other end of the house. Other days I may have been working four twelve-hour night shifts in a row and I fall asleep with the book still in my hand, my mind full of desire to read but my body deciding otherwise. The only thing that really matters is that you do something that truly makes your heart sing and it makes you feel great. I also talk to the children each day about what we are grateful for, we used to write these down and keep them in a jar. As they got older, this became a bit time-consuming at breakfast time, I didn't have the patience for spelling practice over my bowl of overnight oats! So, this is a verbal conversation as we are doing hair and putting shoes on. Easy peasy, no pressure. Winning at the spiritual mum stuff, winning at filling my cup, winning at quality time with the children before school. It is a win-win exercise! So, what are you waiting for? Go forth, and fill your cup! Head on over to the Facebook group and share your ideas on how to fill your cup, you never know who you may inspire with your whacky ways.

As a busy modern woman, there are so many pressures on us to be perfect. I do not think this will ever go away, nor is it unique to our generation, it is just part and parcel of being a woman. It is very easy to drop what is important to us in favour of someone else in our household because somewhere along the line in life we have decided it is selfish to want to do something for ourselves when we have a family to look after. But on the other hand, what happens to that family if you are not at your best? Are you burning yourself out and snapping at the kids before they go off to school in the morning? Stop yourself in your tracks and identify what is happening to you and schedule something in for you, TODAY. If you really do believe that you are too busy to take ten minutes out for your own wellbeing, you are in need of filling your cup more than ever, something needs to change and this requires urgent attention. You have permission to call a rain check on your healthy home-cooked meal tonight, forget the organics and wholefood store on your way home, nip into the local chippy and grab a take-away. Plonk the family down in front of the TV with their beige and beige deli delight, and go off and do something for yourself. No judgement... for me this would be a bath with the door locked (if the damn thing worked!) and a curry pot noodle with just the right amount of sauce! And of course a book in one hand! I said no judgement!

Are you still telling yourself at this moment that you are fine? "I'm fine, totally fine"? Well, Ross said this in season ten of Friends and he was clearly not FINE, and neither are you, you are one margarita away from balance! We can never do enough stuff to fill our cups!

You will know if you are being truthful about the answer to this as you will be either one of two scenarios right now, you have already put the book down and planned something for you today or you are rolling your eyes at the idea of doing something for yourself. Why are you so reluctant to take time out for you? What are you afraid of? Is it your own company, what might you do? There is nothing to-do? You should be spending time with your children, your parents, your partner, your friends. STOP! Just stop it, this guilt does not serve you and will drain your cup, it will drill little holes all over the sides of your cup. You will never give yourself permission to see the value in your own importance if you allow this train of thought to reside in your mindset. Make a change today.

If you are too busy to do something for yourself, ask yourself what are you too busy doing in the first place? Because making time for you can be as simple as taking a longer shower, going to your reading room while the children do their homework, walking to the shop for that loaf of bread instead of driving, leaving for work on the earlier train so you can enjoy some people watching from a café window before you head inside the workplace.

This is not something you can dip in and out of, this is a daily habit to establish and to enjoy for the rest of your life, you can thank me for this tiny nugget of advice later.

> *Great things are done by a series of small things that are brought together.*
>
> — VINCENT VAN GOGH

Please do not ever feel guilty about taking time out

for yourself. Society thrives on fear and guilt, subconsciously we feel the need to succumb to never-ending pressures and fears bestowed upon us by what we read and how others around us act. I implore you to rise above the herd and become your own unique version of you, be selective of the information you allow to permeate your mind and be aware of what drains your cup.

We are busy modern women who are all about 'enjoying all life has to offer' and everything else thrown in for good measure. I want to encourage you to be a tiny bit more selfish or rather, be more self-aware and count yourself as the number one person in your life. Fill your cup with all the goodness that you can, seek it out and engulf your life in heart singing moments.

To be the person that inspires others need not be a laborious chore but a delightful 'gift of giving' to someone else to help them along their life path. Sometimes we feel the pressure of having to know all the answers or to be the one with the uplifting and witty words, this does not need to be the case at all. Inspire those around you by being your true aligned self with an honest smile on your face. Doing this will not only lift those around you without effort but whip them up in a vibrational ecstasy that is addictive to our souls. Your energy is what is felt by people before words are spoken, so keep your cup topped up!

Being able to identify when you are out of alignment with yourself puts you miles ahead of most humans walking this planet. You are developing your emotional intelligence and deepening the connection you have to your true self. The fastest way back to vibrational alignment and a feeling of balance is to regularly keep this line of communication open with yourself. Keep checking in on YOU.

6

GROWTH MINDSET

> *Whether you think you can or think you can't,*
> *you are right.*

— HENRY FORD

I am at risk of being a bit 'mumsie' in this chapter and for those of you who do not have children I would like you to consider the children you are around and potentially influencing through conversations like your nieces and nephews or perhaps your friends children. They may be toddlers or they may be about to head off to University, age does not prevent us from laying the first few foundational thoughts of growth and inspiration. I have had to stop myself from trying to inject inspiration in children that I see at the park struggling with the monkey bars, I want to run over there and tell them, "Whether you believe you can or believe you can't, either way you are right! There is no such word as can't. Failure only happens the moment you quit". That child will then be forever inspired and motivated to challenge themselves at every opportunity, and will remember that crazy lady in the park who came running over with such profound words of wisdom which they never forgot! It's all just a fairy-tale thought, but you never know!

I grew up in the nineties! There was no social media, online influencers, online bullying or mobile phones. (I didn't get my first mobile phone until I was fourteen years old and even then it was a brick!) If I wanted to speak to my bestie Bonnie, I had to cycle to the nearest phone box at the caravan site across the road; the same place I terrorised with the odd handful of shingle chucked on-top of the caravans in the middle of the night, usually during sleepovers camping in the garden with Bonnie! Living in the country invited its own kind of creative fun.

In contrast to the nineties way of life, children nowadays are growing up in a world full of distractions and influences that were not even a 'thing' for a child of my time. The careers list at school today is worlds away from what I was presented with at fourteen years old and making my subject choices for Standard Grades in High School. Think social media influencer, vlogger, virtual assistant, social media consultant, search engine optimization consultant, affiliate marketer, drop shipping reseller. Not a single one of these career choices were money-making opportunities to me growing up in the nineties. You can become anything you want and make money out of it today, bloody hell I am an online mindset coach, what the hell even is that? I get asked that a lot!

Put yourself in a child's shoes for a moment and think about what you would do with such a limitless list of opportunities, but at fourteen you have to decide on subjects at school which will affect your career prospects forever! They see kids their age online, learning to drive in a Tesla, then there is someone else throwing TVs off their parents' many mansion balconies, just to test the strength of Oobleck while earning a fortune for each view and like, and someone else is bragging about becoming a millionaire vlogger on YouTube and someone else has 25K followers on 'The Gram' and has just landed a sponsored holiday to Florida and free tickets to Disney Land. What the hell are they supposed to do with all this information and temptation? Oh so, you are going to ban them from watching YouTube, Snapchat, TikTok, and Instagram. Calm your jets, information is everywhere. It surrounds us. Social media is everything and it is how our children have grown up, we are the ones with the issue with it, not them.

Children are wonderful multitaskers. We need to give them credit for being able to surround themselves in the crazy that is social media, while also figuring out who they are and what they want out of life.

I want to take you on a walk down the garden path of thought and for you to think about a different way of engaging with your children and yourself. Growth mindset is not exclusive for children, I personally use this way of thinking daily and it is a welcome change to our regular fixed way of thinking.

Growth mindset is a learning theory developed by Dr. Carol Dweck which centres around the belief that you can improve intelligence, ability, and performance through the way you approach a problem with your method of thinking. A fixed mindset is often referred to as being a series of thoughts and beliefs which are set in stone with no desire to challenge the thought. A growth mindset is trained to look for an opportunity for improvement and failure is not feared but celebrated for the learning opportunities it brings forward.

There is so much possibility when it comes to

discussing the words we say to ourselves or each other which inspire us to think in a different way. And this is all growth mindset is really; using an alternative collection of words put together which suggests a different way of thinking.

Let me give you some examples of how this translates.

- Fixed mindset – I can't do it.
- Growth mindset – I can not do it yet.
- Fixed mindset – I give up.
- Growth mindset – I'll try a different way.
- Fixed mindset – I made a mistake.
- Growth mindset – Mistakes help me learn.
- Fixed mindset – It's good enough.
- Growth mindset – Is this really my best work?

Come up with your own growth mindset alternatives to the following fixed mindset phrases and explore how the alternative collection of words make you feel.

- This is too hard.
- I'll never complete this on time.
- I'm not clever enough to apply.
- I always come last.
- I don't like doing this.

- What is the point in going any further?

There are no limitations to the growth aspect of the discussion, its sole purpose is to challenge and inspire an alternative thought process. If we are not challenging ourselves on our thinking and behaviour regularly, are we really growing in the direction we wish to go? I often think about the ways in which I was taught and spoken to as a child; how my thinking or understanding of the world could have been enhanced and could I have learned more about a situation if I had been encouraged to think with a growth mindset? Not just by what was given to me by a parent or a teacher. This is something I ask myself daily and something I would like to inspire you to cast a thought over. Do you speak to yourself in a fixed mindset? Do you encourage the children in your life by the words you offer them to exercise their problem-solving minds? If not or this is new thinking for you, make the change today.

Giving ourselves the confidence to explore our awareness and how our minds work when faced with day to day problems really encourages our minds to build resilience and curiosity. It is the same for the children in our lives. From my years of studying and practicing the law of attraction and self-development I have learned that it all starts with knowing yourself and trusting your instincts; finding out what feels good to you. Any encouragement to think in this way at any age is a big yes in my opinion.

When I think about the effect other people will have on my children throughout their childhood, I have to admit it does put me on edge sometimes, especially when the conversation is centred around a topic which I feel can be fragile when building the foundations of understanding, for example money mindset, belief of ability, academic grading, etcetera. I often find myself having a debrief with my children when I feel they have been party to a particularly fixed mindset perspective leading the conversation. Despite this neurotic approach to the mindset of my children, which I am fully aware I am over-thinking or rather let me say I am airing on the side of caution; there are areas of influence out of our control like school, friends, and what they view online. Yes, you could home school your children and limit their screen to time to that which you monitor or share with them, but it is fair to say that our children will want to explore beyond the boundaries we set for them. That is OK providing we can equip them with the confidence to deal with what they may face on their journey to adulthood and beyond, or the odd de-brief from time to time if we feel they have been corrupted by the fixed mindset brigade!

Having an attitude of gratitude has exploded my

children's understanding of what is important to them and how they perceive anything to be. They are growing to understand that to see life through the eyes of love and not fear or stress makes them happy. Meditation, mindfulness, growth mindset are all great tools to equip ourselves with.

7

RETURN TO LOVE

Love is not what you say.
Love is what you do.

We have reached my favourite chapter and the topic of my development which is ever-evolving and to be completely transparent with you, one which took some time to understand and appreciate, despite learning that the truest emotion of all is that of love.

Some say we do not fall in love or experience love until at first our heart is broken for the first time. Others will argue that we are born feeling only love for that is the truest feeling of all. We are not born knowing anger or discord, we learn this from our experiences as we grow. Love is when we are at our purest vibrational place. Have you ever heard the saying, 'Love conquers all'? Returning to love brings this to life.

Sometimes the airy-fairiness of spirituality switches my mind off. I am guessing this might be the same for you, so I want to make spirituality cool, and for you to feel that it is ok to say that you are exploring or embracing your spirituality without mumbling it under your breath and rushing passed the topic when asked. Feel empowered by the words. I used to misunderstand spirituality for religion, and this made me contract. I am not a religious person nor am I an atheist. I am an open-minded individual who has a deep desire to embrace that part of me that I cannot see, but who is me and so much more. I implore you to do the same.

Coming back to love is a habit to practice as it is the fastest way back to emotional balance. Returning to love is widely written about in books across many genres so you may already be aware of this insight. I am not going to smokescreen this lesson as it is a challenge to embrace. We do not naturally want to return to love when something has upset us, our years of social conditioning have made sure of that. Despite our instinctive emotion when we are born is that of love, it is chipped away through the years and can leave us feeling unloved, hateful, resentful, and anxious. To unlearn a lifetime of habit is not easy but not impossible. The Chinese proverb "Be not afraid of growing slowly, be afraid only of standing still" is rather perceptive and encourages me to start with the smallest of steps.

What does it mean to return to love? Well, let me start by explaining the vibration of our thoughts and feelings. Our entire Universe vibrates. Every atom in every 'thing' vibrates. Everything we see, touch, think and feel is ENERGY. Energy vibrates at different frequencies and the Law of Attraction is the universal law that explains it. Energy vibrating at a certain frequency will attract more energy of that same vibration. The Law of Attraction matches vibrations with like vibrations which are the basis of the expansion of our Universe, in a nutshell.

The vibration of love is very pure and incredibly healing and the true vibration of our soul. We are not born full of hate, nor are we born with worry or judgement. We learn these emotions. Our true emotion is that of LOVE. Try your best not to resist this, allow these words to flow and embrace the feelings which surface as you read them.

The tough bit I found was returning to love when someone had pissed me off, judged me, wronged me; I found it challenging to return to love when I was triggered into fight mode. How can you see love when someone has crapped on your proverbial cornflakes? It takes time and you need to allow yourself to take a step back from the situation for a moment or two while you break the emotional trigger which is wanting to send all the guns blazing. Think about where it came from, why it has triggered you and in the moment allow the emotion to rise to the surface and then ease into balance through observation and love. Feeling love for yourself in this moment, understanding that a negative exchange of words is an eruption of energy and not constructive. When you feel the pressure rising, engage your mind and to allow it to pass and feel love instead.

We are all a work in progress, some are further along on that journey than others and some will find a certain aspect to their development easier than others. Returning to love is notoriously challenging for many of us as it can feel like forgiveness masquerading as acceptance, this is absolutely not the case. Forgiveness and acceptance are completely different and surprisingly low vibration, as the feeling is masked and the root cause is ignored. The vibration of love has a much higher frequency and it is our instinctive emotional state. We have simply just forgotten this.

I am not an outwardly lovey-dovey person. I find it very challenging to express the emotion of love, I feel deeply embarrassed and vulnerable and I have learned that this feeling is rooted in the fear of rejection and this is something I am working on as part of my personal spiritual development. In recent years I have worked with two wonderful energy healers, a husband and wife team called Oliva and Raf Ocana (links to connect with them can be found at the back) and they helped me heal a very troubling time I was having with Trev. They taught me how to return to love and how powerful the healing would be if I could surrender myself to the embrace of love.

Let me give you a little context to the problem as it may resonate with you. (I touched on Trev's accident in the introduction and mentioned that we had a challenging time in the years to come, well this was a make or break situation for us.) We struggled for years to get the help we needed to rehabilitate, not only for him personally, but as a family and as a couple. After his accident, life was very different from how it used to be, and we had to learn how to navigate the minefield of emotions and triggers that could potentially become a two-week fight. Oliva and Raf helped me to understand what it meant to return to love. I had read about returning to love a couple of years before in the book by Gabrielle Bernstein 'The Universe Has Your Back', but I just couldn't figure out how to apply it to my relationship when things became prickly. Olivia and Raf taught me to step outside of my emotional state and see a larger view of the situation which had become the main focus of my attention. I was encouraged to be compassionate, even if I felt I had been wronged or felt upset; to look for a reason as to why I was being verbally attacked. There is always a reason even if you cannot see it initially your job in this situation is to be kind, listen and hear the other person. I understand this is incredibly difficult to do, but from my experience it brought any argument down from a fortnight of silence and grunting to an evening of conversation and understanding. I was flabbergasted by the miraculous results of becoming open and seeing love, not anger. Even if you have a point to make, discuss that point at a later moment, your job is not to be right or to win the argument. Your job is to take the fizz out of the situation and return to love as fast as you can.

When I stopped arguing and trying to prove my point, when I began to listen to why Trev was upset with me or the world in general, I heard him. I could see what had triggered him from a different perspective. There is that word again, perspective. It is really powerful. Do not ever forget the power you have when viewing from another perspective. I could feel love in my understanding, in his words, in the resolution; the healing follows quickly from this. It is not in the physical act of love, although that is important, the vibration of love is undisguisable. You feel it, even if you do not know what you are feeling, if the person beside you is vibrating at the frequency of love, it is way more powerful than the frequency of anger.

If your learning is enhanced by visual storytelling, I would urge you to pop over to YouTube and check out a Japanese scientist called Masaru Emoto and his experiment on water consciousness. It is mind-blowing. He also has a book called 'The Hidden Messages in Water' which details the effects our emotional vibration has on water and when the results are discovered it is absolutely breath-taking, you will be blown away by the outcome.

8

IT IS OK TO SAY NO

> *By saying yes when you need to say no, you cripple the most important relationship in your life: the relationship between you and you.*

— UNKNOWN

Do you find it easy to say no? Or are you an obsessive people-pleaser who hates the idea of rejecting a fellow human regardless of the request? Be honest with yourself. I used to fall into this category until I learned the art of saying no; trust me it was easier than I expected because the benefits came quick and fast, and you know what? Not one single person took offence nor did the world implode because I said no to a simple ask from a friend! We need to learn to get over ourselves and stop this need of pleasing others before ourselves. Remember the chapter on 'Fill your cup'? Flick back and refresh yourself if you are reading through the book slowly to remind yourself of the importance of your self-care. Filling your cup and saying no complement each other.

You are the guardian of your own time and your happiness. We are all granted 24 hours every day to farm this experience for ourselves. Now having covered the aspect of time in the first chapter, I now want you to remind yourself that using the excuse of having no time to fulfil whatever request has come your way is simply not enough. Having read this book now negates the ability to ever use the excuse, I do not have time. But as we are here to grow and learn it is ok to feel resistance towards this thinking; you are never the finished result of your progress, every day is a day for improvement and every day has the opportunity for growth. If you find yourself needing to rethink your words, that is OK. The mastery is in the awareness of how you think.

When we act from a feeling of expectation or obligation, in that very moment you are telling your subconscious mind that you are not the most important person in your life, that it is OK for you to take a backseat and become the onlooker in your own life. Now I hate to state the obvious, but for the sake of those who will feel compelled to shout at me to tell me that their kids always come first and I am talking shit, let me stop you there. I whole-heartedly agree, kids always come first. Period. I am talking about the requests from those outsides of your four walls. Requests from friends, neighbours, work, family, and the pressure you put on yourself to be the one who can do it all, this category is where we shall focus our attention.

I was a serial people pleaser; I did not actually know it was a 'thing' until I was watching Friends and Monica was talking about her uncontrollable need to please people. The words jumped through the screen and slapped me across the face. I had no idea I was doing it, I thought it was just being a good friend. I make it sound like I was a really needy friend. I wasn't, I just made myself far too available for other people and rarely prioritised myself or my personal space. Not long after this, I saw a Ted Talk by Mel Robbins and I had a moment of clarity. I was giving up valuable time for myself on people who were not valuing me and for those who would not do the same in return. Now, this is not to say you do anything in life to expect acknowledgement at some point, what I mean is that by being so free with my time and energy it became expected of me; I was holding on to the wrong energy around my wellbeing. I wanted to be seen as a 'good' friend. I felt it was selfish or flaky to let a friend down or to be unavailable.

When it comes to your children there is no need to be bold and say no to their emotional desires, of course say no to them wanting to go to the shop naked, wearing only their trampolining socks (the specifics in the detail shine a tiny glimpse into my morning today!), I mean don't say no to the things that support their emotional development like will you play a game with me? Can we have a chat about something I just saw on YouTube? Can you read to me? Lap up these requests. There is all the time in the world for this relationship to grow, even if it means putting down what you think is important at the time. Nothing is more important than the wellbeing of a child.

I started to take on board some of the advice that I had learned from Mel in her Ted Talk and I began to prioritise myself and my energy. It became easy to say no to stuff that did not make my heart sing. It became incredibly empowering to say no and not feel the need to follow it up with some cosmetic excuse to prevent offence. Sometimes I would walk away muttering, "Fuck it, what's the worst that can happen?" under my breath to keep me feeling true to my rebellious self!

Just to be clear, I have not become a super-bitch! I

am the same delightful person, just without the neediness! I love to make people happy and to be a kind and helpful friend, only now I do this without compromising my energy. Did I lose any friends along the way? No, I did not. There is nothing to fear by saying no. If anything, it actually boosted the relationships I already had, as I gave myself more value and this became clear in my behaviour and my body language.

For so many of us time is a huge factor when it comes to making positive changes in our lives or more specifically, not having enough of it. Reading that book, signing up for that course, meditation, and journaling all require an investment of time. Start saying no to one or two things a week that would free up some time and energy for you. Take a look at your week, what can you say no to? Freeing up your mind will allow your energy to flow so much more freely around you and enable you to do more of what makes your heart sing. If you can allow yourself a degree of honesty with this, you will find there are plenty of things in your week you can say no to.

When you shift your mindset onto you and your value, what you spend your time on then feels different. Be a great friend, yes. A great sister, yes. A great partner, yes. But be mindful of being the best version of you that you can be. This will always mean allowing change of some description to happen. Saying no once in a while does not mean you do not love the person who is asking for your time. You are quite simply placing more value on you and your energy, and this is ok. Do not let anyone make you feel guilty for it. If not yet, then in time you will see the magic that manifests by saying no.

It is essential for your mindset that you spend time with those who value you and doing the things that make your heart sing. Nurture your soul by being true to you and if you feel like just saying no, follow that intuition and do just that. Who cares if it means you are changing your mind at the last minute? Trust this feeling for it does not stay around for long. Moments after our intuition makes us think our thoughts or feel our feelings, our ego begins talking us down from being spontaneous. Sparking feelings of doubt, fear, indecisiveness, and worry. It takes time to master the acknowledgment of the presence of the ego vs our intuition.

Let me try something with you. In a moment I am going to ask you a direct question. I want you to be aware of your answer the moment you 'hear' it within your consciousness. This is the very first thought that pops into your mind upon reading the question, not the one you think you should be thinking! I see you over there over-thinker!

Ok here goes...

"Where would you love to be right now?"

Right there, that first thought, not the one you are trying to make appear like the one you want to hear, the first one, the raw one. Not where do you think you should be, or where do your kids want to go. This is all about you and hearing your intuition. The very first answer is the one I want you to get into the habit of looking for. Ignoring all the ego BS that comes up afterward. Get familiar with your first thoughts, whether it makes perfect sense to you or not. The first thought that came to me when I typed those words was sitting on my mum and dad's chocolate brown leather sofa in the kitchen eating ice cream! My ego wants to challenge this because for one, I do not really like ice cream and two, I want to think of being somewhere tropical and relaxing! The idea behind all this is that you practice asking yourself questions and listen for the intuitive answer. Notice when your ego tries to overtake and argue with your intuitive senses. You need to learn to stifle your ego when it pops up like this.

Use this style of questioning whenever you are faced with an opportunity for you to do something that does not prioritise your happiness. Now it must be noted here that this is not about questioning your friendships or level of commitment to any one person, it is simply allowing you to free up your energy around the activities and the people you spend your time with. This may fluctuate and that is completely fine. When you make decisions from this place of alignment within you, you are bringing forth the spiritual change which you so desire. This empowerment will make your heart sing.

Saying no is not a comfortable thing for many people to say, but when you leave it up to the Universe to decide for you by way of asking your intuitive self, you can take the ownership of guilt or disappointment away from saying no to someone. Blame the Universe! I have a friend who tells people (when she wants to say no to them), "Aw babes, I am just not energetically aligned to this idea!" She is a real spiritual hippy! The shit she comes out with makes me laugh so much.

This single change in your mindset will allow you to become more aligned with your inner self. You will feel so much more confident within your relationships and friendships and you will feel like a winner of time. You will no longer find yourself taking part in this, that, and the next when all you really want to be doing is spending your one free afternoon alone at home while everyone else happens to be out and you have, dare I say it, A FREE DAY! Saying no need not bring about guilt. Saying no is empowering and you are telling yourself that you value you, your time, your energy, and you will only spend it on the things that truly make your heart sing.

Let go of any feeling that by saying no you are being selfish or rude. Let go of any need to justify your answer. A simple no said with a smile and a thank you is all you need to equip yourself with.

How does this make you feel in principle? Are you all fired up and equipped with the word no on the tip of your tongue ready for the first person to request your presence? Let me run through a couple of scenarios with you. I would like to invite you to practice saying no to these scenarios. If they mean nothing to you, make up your own relevant alternative to situations. The idea behind it is to experience feeling the liberation of saying no. Picture what you would do with the time instead.

- Going out for midweek drinks with work/mum/uni friends?
- Booking a holiday with the same friends again next year?
- Looking after Suzie's children after school every Thursday?
- Being the designated driver on the girl's night out AGAIN?
- Going back to the same hairstylist after years of her not getting your hair quite right?
- What are your fears around saying no? What

might they think? What will you do with the time instead?

You have permission to say no the next time you feel compelled to say yes. Your happiness is your responsibility, take ownership of it.

9

YOU'VE CHANGED!

You really haven't changed; you have just become more of yourself. That is really what we are all trying to do: become more of ourselves.

— OPRAH WINFREY

I am fairly confident in assuming that almost all of us at some time or another have received the 'accusation' "You've changed". I say accusation here because it has negative connotations to it disguised as a question of curiosity from a loved one. (Don't let anyone tell you otherwise!)

"You've changed" is so condescending yet it remarkably attempts to pass itself off as being inquisitive. People love to identify when you no longer fit with them and try to put you down assive-aggressively by using this phrase. I remember when someone said it to me, I recall feeling confused by the remark in my eyes I had not changed, I was still the person I always was but my lifestyle was different from how it was when we had spent time together previously. This comment that my so-called 'friend' had left on a Facebook post I had shared really stuck with me for a while, I questioned myself at the time. Why did I feel so bad? Why was she shaming me so publicly on social media?

As humans we naturally group together, we need to be liked and accepted by our peers, it is in our DNA. We do not like to be singled out no matter how independent we claim to be. I am that person who claims to need no-one else. "I am a lone wolf and I don't care what other people think of me". This statement itself cries out for the need of acceptance. I need to be accepted. I need to be liked. I need to be laughed with. I need to be wanted. But I will say repeatedly that I do not care what other people think of me. It is my shield! If I say, "I don't care", then the conversation stops, and I can deflect my need for attention onto something else less painful. The feeling of rejection can overwhelm us and send us into an emotional tailspin, questioning everything we think we know about ourselves.

Let me tell you something, writing this book has

been the single most painful, soul grating, and tear-jerking process I could have ever imagined. I have shared a part of me that I have never spoken aloud, I have faced the inner darkness and challenged my ability; I fear the fact that this book will sit on the shelves of homes around the world for the lifetime of its enjoyment and purpose, open to criticism, open to judgement, open to rejection; I fear the day I find it on the bookshelf in my local charity shop. I honestly fear its success probably more than its failure if you can believe that. Yes, a mindset coach who is afraid of success! Allow me the honesty of that statement, there is more to come on this.

When someone says to you, "You've changed" they are, in the simplest of words, expressing a fear within them that they no longer fit with you and that maybe you won't like them anymore; maybe your friendship has been brought into question and this makes them feel unloved. Whatever the trigger for this know and trust that it is not a 'you' problem, this is a 'them' problem. Respond with love as always but be mindful of your energy. Do not allow yourself to get dragged down by this, know your heart and your truth, be free of any mood hoovering at a time like this.

- Change is positive.
- Change is natural.

- Change is universal.
- Change is growth.
- Change is powerful.
- Change is unstoppable.

Embrace the change which you recognise within yourself, encourage change within you at every opportunity for this is where you will experience your biggest growth. People will be people and people will forever try and bring one another down. Allow yourself to be different, to make positive choices to become the person you want to be and know you can be. Allow change into your life as scary as it may seem at the time; when making inspired decisions for ourselves trust that the change that follows is true and aligned, just for you right in that very moment in time. Everything is working out just as it should. Do not allow anyone to tell you otherwise.

It is OK for others around you to feel scared that a change within you may threaten them. It raises a feeling of uncertainty in their minds and the feeling of rejection is prominent for them prompting a possible undesirable response. Again, this is a 'them' problem. Remember this when you feel that you are experiencing emotions that are conflicting with you at the time. Resist the temptation to get into an argument or justify yourself to anyone. Be true to yourself and give only love. Conversation and compassion are key to the evolution of our relationships.

How you handle a situation will ultimately determine your feelings about it and as I have mentioned previously it is always the faster and smoother road down the path of love. Always love, despite how difficult it may seem at the time. Your friends love you and are merely displaying an emotional trigger by telling you that they can see a change in you. Reassure your loved one by telling them how much they mean to you, explain that you are focusing more on the things that make your heart sing. Tell them what you love about your relationship together without justifying yourself. Challenge their words with love, love is always the best way.

You've changed is just another way of someone telling you that you have stopped living your life, their way. Responding to someone who has announced that "You've changed" is where you can call your power and negate the feeling of rejection or judgement that you may be experiencing. Try some of these suggestions on for size.

- Thanks for noticing!
- Are you suggesting that change is a bad thing?

- It was time for me to make some personal improvements.
- I read a book and it changed my life.
- Change is inevitable.
- We are all changing, it is really not all that scary.
- Thank goodness I have.
- I would like to think so, I am 35 now!

However you respond to someone's comments directed at you always be kind and come from a place of love, no matter how much your default reaction is to verbally destroy them. Only love, love, love! (if you are humming the song, I am not even sorry!)

Jim Rohn talked a lot about human connections and their intertwining relationships, he said, "You are the average of the five people you spend the most time with". What do you think when reading that? The first time I ever read these words my thoughts exploded, I questioned everyone around me; I wasn't sure if I was to factor in my children because at the time my children were very little and I was a full-time mum. My eyes must have bulged from their sockets in shock. How was I to evaluate my mindset based on the people I was gauging my average on. It did make me laugh and worry in equal measure until I saw beyond the fog and realised what this statement allowed me to survey. This was not a judgement of my home life or mothering ability, this was an evaluation of the perception of my reality, my friendships, my peers, my self-worth. Did I surround myself with people who lifted me up, encouraged me, loved me, laughed with me, helped me grow? Or did I allow myself to fall short of what I wanted from my friendships? Was I a waste product of the negative reflection of the flaws I had seen in others? Was I becoming more judgemental because of too much time together over coffee? 'The average of the five people I spent the most time with' quite possibly was the first time I took a good look at myself in the mirror and saw the desire for deep spiritual growth. I wanted to become all types of good in this world during my human experience and this statement was just what I needed to push me on my way. This inevitably marked the beginning of significant change emerging for me and it has ruffled a few feathers along the way, but nothing that the words of love can't heal.

It makes you think though, do you behave, talk, or act in a certain way around certain people? Whose mindset are you twenty percent of? Humans are born mimics of each other. We behave in this way to gain the approval of others, to fit in, to be accepted by our peers. Have you ever spent time in another English-speaking country for a considerable amount of time and found yourself starting to adopt a different accent? Several years ago, I moved to New Zealand so I could experience 'backpacking' although there was no backpack in sight! I was a suitcase traveller and I found myself in Australia for a further twelve months after spending a year in New Zealand. I could hear my soft and subtle Scottish accent as it turned Kiwi for me to 'fit in'. Some of the words that I used changed as fast as within the first week because no one knew what I was talking about when I said flip flops, they are called jandals in New Zealand and peppers were not peppers, they were capsicums! My first ever trip to Subway was a mind-blowing experience and not just for me, my server was quite taken aback by my blue Scottish skin colour and my flip flops and my request for peppers in my salad. And my mobile phone was no longer a mobile, I had a cell phone! I did all this subconsciously to fit in with the people around me. I did not think about it until I stumbled upon a new traveller and we got talking about the funny word swaps! After two years of being 'Down Under' I came home sounding like I was straight out of Ramsay Street and I had to unlearn all the words to fit in with my friends and family back home again. I became a chameleon. I felt shamed on my return home after the two years with my 'funny accent', the comments began to come in about the way I spoke and how I sounded back in Inverness. "You are not living in Australia any more Claire". It almost seems petty to write about it now, but it is sympathetic to the feeling of shame that someone can put on you when they feel like you don't fit in with them anymore. If we allow ourselves to be adaptable and change as the situation demands and which suits us energetically, this feeling of rejection that comes from changing a part of our being can be released and allow us to bring that wonderful vibration of balance into our lives.

10

GOAL SETTING

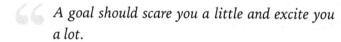 *A goal should scare you a little and excite you a lot.*

— JOE VITALE

Can you remember a day when you jumped in your car, pressed your foot to the gas and hurtled out of your driveway into the unknown? You literally had no idea where you are driving to, you are just driving for the sake of driving, wasting fuel, passing time, looking at the scenery as it passes by. I expect that for many of you reading this book the answer to this will be NEVER.

Think about this in terms of your life. Are you living life hoping for the best and bouncing from one experience to another? Where are you headed? What do you want to achieve? What do you want to experience and encounter? How do you know if you have achieved the things you desire if you do not know what they are in the first place?

Let me share something personal and painful about me, raw and stripped back. Someone very close to me once said during a conversation we were engaged in about an idea I had for a future business, "Come on Claire, it's hard to take you seriously when you never see anything through, you always stop and start stuff, you never do the things you say you are going to do". These words hit me like a tonne of bricks. They penetrated my soul and tarnished my self-belief. And in all honesty, I have allowed these words to hold me back for most of my adult life. I have given those words unbelievable power by feeding into the belief that I am flaky and inconsistent and that I lack passion and direction. It has given me the excuse to quit when the tough times hit me, because what is the point in breaking the habit of a lifetime? No need to exert yourself Claire, you do not succeed at anything anyway so no need to try and surprise anyone, and let's face it, nobody likes surprises.

This clouded belief I had in myself was not mine, it was someone else's which I listened to and I believed. I made it personal because it hurt me so much, it was such a powerful emotional trigger for me. Why did I do this? Honestly?

It was because I did not have a life goal. Not one single goal.

I did not have my life map planned out.

I did not have the postcode of success to enter into my life nav.

I knew that I was bumbling about in the dark without any real clue what I was doing or where I was going. Worse still, I knew that the person who said this to me could see within me that I was lacking something in my direction. So, it must simply be true mustn't it? This would be the story I told myself repeatedly whenever I would look at my life and wonder what was happening.

A goal without a plan is just a wish.

I have spent much of my life a stranger to the idea of setting goals; far be it for me to want something to happen to me which is far bigger and greater than I currently have. I have always been content with my plate to a degree. Yes, I could argue that I would look at the grass on the other side and say it looked greener on occasions, but I was never engaged in a train of thought that would allow me to believe I could change my life. I was not wired up psychologically to think like that, or indeed believe that it was even possible.

The first time I ever engaged in thinking about PLANNING a bigger life for myself was in 2014. I had just started my very first business and I was asked by someone who was helping me put an action plan in place for the growth of my business "What are your goals, Claire?". Now for the risk of sounding like an absolute fool, I had no idea about growth or planning, structure, or expansion. I had absolutely no idea what my goals were. When asked what made me excited about the future, I couldn't answer because I had no idea; I had never in my life thought about my future in a structured manner, in actual fact the idea brought out an anxiety in me. I was scared I would come across greedy or materialistic if I agreed to the suggestions she was putting to me, financial freedom (whatever that means to you) life without limits, whatever that meant? The white Range Rover to drive my kids to private school with their perfect little hats on, God NO!! None of this stuff made my heart sing. I would later learn why this method of questioning did not resonate with me or unveil the desires which were hidden among my consciousness.

Everyone is different and we each set goals in vastly different ways, so there is no right or wrong way to get that road map planned out. If you want to create a bigger and better life full of all the things you want to experience you need to be clear with yourself about what they are in the first place.

Knowing which way suits you best makes goal setting so much easier. I am a 'Process' goal setter. I very much like to have an idea of where I am going, it is free to change as inspiration sees fit, so I focus my attention upon the action I take to get there, enjoying the feeling of fulfilment I get from the small things along the way, one new liker, one new reader on my blog, this all feels good to me. I know what I am aiming towards and the journey there is full of celebrating the small wins.

The 'Outcome' goal setter would likely feel frustrated and disheartened by that slow but steady growth, it is all about the end result for you. You may even have a date and time attached to your goal. For those of you who are process goal-setters, time limits and heavy deadlines will send you straight into the corner of the room rocking and sweating.

What I would love to do through this chapter is to inspire you to think about your own life and what you want from it. If this is a completely new way of thinking for you it can be a rather daunting prospect to map your life out with things you want to become, experience, and own. If you are holding yourself back because of what people might think about your goals, I can sympathise as I am exactly the same. I hate the idea of people knowing what I am setting my sights on. I am a very private person and the idea of someone else knowing my big goals makes me contract. For now, you have permission to keep it a secret. You do not need to advertise your vision board on social media or even on your living room wall if you do not want to. If it is super personal for you that is perfectly ok. The worst thing for me was the thought of someone knowing what I wanted and being held to my words, the pressure and fear of failure that bubbled to the surface every time I would think about or glance at an image on my vision board that represented that goal was overbearing.

One of my first experiences of this 'pressure' was in my early days as a new entrepreneur. I was in a network of 'work from home' people. I was being coached on how to use social media to expand my network and falling into the whole idea of attraction marketing. I now cringe at the thought of conducting myself in such a way, I was being so blindly led by others who were seemingly successful around me: "Do what I do and you will get the same results as me, look at my social media life, it's so perfect"! I really was that fucking desperate!

I was completely new to all this goal setting stuff and I had no idea what it was that I really wanted out of life, besides a happy family and a happy home. Material things did not hold a great deal of value to me and I thought there was something wrong with me because of this. Everyone around me was putting private school uniforms, images of Range Rovers, images of wads of cash up on their goal boards and by the looks of social media, these things were manifesting themselves into other people's lives quickly. One woman even watched Grand Designs one night, saw a house she loved, googled it, found out it was around the corner from her current home, stuck it on her vision board and then moved into it within six months. It was like real-life adult magic; I was hypnotised by the majestic power these vision boards seemed to have.

I was reeling, nothing magical was happening to me so I asked for some help from one of these people who seemed to be drinking from the so-called 'magic fountain'. She told me to pick a car I would like to drive one day and go and arrange a test drive, and take Trev with me to let him feel the magic of the experience too so he can get behind the business, oh and take lots of photos, "Get a good one for social media". OK I thought that seems easy enough, so I called Range Rover and I booked a test drive (because everyone seemed to want one of these, perhaps the company had some special deal with them and it would be easier to get than say, a fucking

Nissan Micra!). We turned up on the day looking like the fucking Flintstones. Trev had chosen to wear his most cherished tracksuit, to this day I still do not know how I did not notice this before we left the house, it was not until we got out of our Vauxhall Vectra (which in those moments felt like the Flintmobile and that I had foot peddled it all the way from my house) when I noticed his ensemble, I could have jumped straight back into my Flintmobile and peddled all the way home had it not been for the promise of the magic photo that was going to make this all manifest into real life. In hindsight, I wish I had because what was about to happen is far too cringeworthy!

We took the drive, and all went well; it was nice but not that spectacular. I did not get that heart skipping moment I was promised I would feel. The posed photo was taken and then... plastered all over social media, even now as I type these words I can feel the reluctance in my fingers to share the story, it hurts to remember how naïve I was! I was, for want of a better word, brainwashed into this materialistic mindset, which is so far from who I am, my true self cannot even be seen. What then followed on from this ridiculous public display of lies were two conversations that I can still recall today, and both stir up negative vibrations for me. One made me feel shame because, "Who was I to go for a test drive in such a fancy car when I did not even have a *proper job*"? The other conversation was more prolonged over time and I was reminded of it regularly each time we spoke. "Tell me, Claire, when is it you are going to be owning this fancy car then? I want to be driven around like Royalty when I come to visit you!" It came from a place of love and a tiny bit of selfishness! But it did not half make me feel like a failure each time I told her it was not happening yet. Each year that photo would pop up as a memory on social media and bring back all those feelings of crrrrringe that I felt on the day I posted it in the first place (only heightened by a million fucking trillion) as I was no closer to owning a Range Rover then as I was the day I test-drove it. That photo has since been deleted and erased forevermore from my social media, but the memory is still there, imprinted deeply like a fossil in my mind, forever reminding me that, *I do not share shit like that on social media,* nor does Claire get emotionally triggered by material objects. This is not to say that material objects or goals are in any way a negative thing, they just do not trigger me into action or create that emotional get up and go.

The opposite of a material goal is an experience-based goal. Think about time freedom, travel, a feeling of accomplishment, respect, good health. I am not suggesting that you have to choose which side of the fence you must sit on, you can by all means be driven by both styles of goal setting and this is helpful to read and understand. You do not have to fit into one box; I felt like I had to choose between one way or the other and because I did not know if one way was more magical than the other, I was so confused and over-thought the whole process. I did not understand what it meant to dig these desires out from my mind or indeed what they looked like when they did surface. How would I know if it was the 'right' goal for me? I hope you find it helpful to read my experience with discovering desire, because for some of us, it does not come easily, but understanding the difference can really help to set you on the right path.

Overthinking goal setting will hinder you from taking action of any shape or form. Have you ever heard the saying procrastination is the enemy of progress? It is so absolutely true.

How to discover your goals or desires.

It all starts with the first step. Get the paper out and reach for a pen and just start writing down things that excite you. Let your mind flow and write anything that comes to your thoughts, just write it all down for now. This is just a brain dumping process and a really helpful activity for unearthing desire or to balance an overthinking mind. The words that feel really good to you as you write them note them down. When I say *feel good*, I mean it makes your heart sing at the thought of it, not simply that it would be lovely for it to happen one day, but makes your heart smile and ache at the sheer thought of it becoming your reality. You may find yourself writing things down that you think you should, you will know this when it happens as you will not have that pang of excitement when you put the words down on paper.

It does not matter what the goal is if it is important to you and it makes your heart sing. If by the end of this process you only have two or three things written down, but you can honestly say that those two or three goals all make you want to jump up and high-five your future self on its physical manifestation, then that is all that matters. You will find more will come to you as you get comfortable with the process.

The brain dumping process is cathartic and it is honest. No one need ever see your brain dump, this can be your completely personal secret process that helps you to become a bigger and better version of yourself. After all, we are here on this earth to grow and become the best version of yourself you can visualise for yourself. Growth is inevitable, but to grow in the direction of your conscious choice is to live a life of fulfilment.

Some people like to create a vision board or a magic box. A vision board is a place for all your goals to live in picture form that you see every day and can visualise yourself having manifested it into your reality. You can see immediately what your goals are without having to take the time to read a list of words. The magic box is just that, a box which you put your goals into and you let them go to the Universe, you just get to work on the action and alignment and you are good to go! There is a deeper science which comes into play here which I am not even going to try to understand, all I can share with you is that having a clear goal set in your mind is halfway to achieving it.

So, what's next?

You now have a list of your goals. To begin the magic process, you need to deposit them into your magic box and let the Universe do what the Universe does best. Or if you would rather see your goals right in front of you as a constant reminder and a force for encouragement get those words turned into images and create a vision board. This can cause the over-thinker to go into overdrive.

What if you can't find the right image?

What if you end up manifesting the exact image you print off and that's not the one you really want, but you couldn't find a perfect match on google?

This was me, I stopped myself from doing anything with my goal setting or vision board because I did not have the pretty tiny paper bunting from Hobby Craft to make my vision board look 'cute'. I had no idea what I even wanted as this magic seemed all too real, it was a risky game for me to play. I then discovered the magic box method, and this changed the world for me! I could keep up my secret squirrel disguise and hold my deepest darkest desires for world domination locked up in my magic chest!

My vision board used to be on the reverse side of a cereal box. Pictures stuck on there with glue or sticky tape, no fancy corner edgings or cute bits of paper bunting. Just pictures and words. It served its purpose and it was functional but it was a trigger for me, seeing my goals so proudly staring me in the face every day and having to discuss them on days with my children or my other half when our life seemed so far away from them was counter-productive for me and I began to lose faith in my ability to achieve them. The complete opposite to what a vision board is supposed to do, but for my secret squirrel personality it was a nightmare. I needed something that was a sure bet for Universal manifestation but for no one else to know about it unless I chose to share my secrets with them. I am a keeper of boxes, all sorts of boxes, not as obsessive as the guy who ordered everything from Amazon in order to collect all the boxes in their repertoire, but I do like a box. Put me in the storage section in Ikea and I will get super stressed about which box to buy, to the point I will probably end up buying none and come home to wallpaper a cereal box instead. But of all the boxes I have chosen as my magic box, it is a gorgeous little antique glass trinket box which I bought from the charity shop a few years ago and it sat for long enough with bobbles, kirby grips and odd earrings in it, but it was too good for such menial drivel, it had magical powers and it had an air of mystic about it.

The magic box is simple, you keep an aligned belief in the goals you deposit into it and let the Universe do what it does best, giving you more of what you feel at your core, what you vibrate. Hold the energy high around your goals and trust that it is only a matter of time before they become your reality, stay focused on what you want to become and on each and every goal you put into that box. Check in on it from time to time, re-read your goals and refresh your enthusiasm for them. Add new goals as often as you like and discard the ones you have moved away from focus. Keep your magic box somewhere that you can see it, so every time you look at it you surge with gratitude over the manifestation of your goals. Even on the shittiest of days, view your box as a magical chest which oozes positivity and hope and a place to recharge your energy. Do not ever doubt your ability to reach your goals, but do remember, in order to know if you have reached it you must have a clear vision of what it is you are aiming for.

If you're a vision board kinda gal but you're not sure how to effectively create one, it is super simple. Start with the first goal you have written down and jump on over to google, search for an image that resonates with your goal in mind, scroll until you find one that speaks to you then repeat this for the rest of your goals. I tend to use a collage app to put pictures from google onto, so I can make them the size I want for my board and print several on one sheet of A4, do my wee bit to save the planet! Now once you have your vision board put it somewhere you are going to see it. Do not hide it away through fear or guilt. Put it in a place which you can spend time looking at it each day. Allow your mind to be in those images, let them come to life, convince yourself that it is only a matter of time until this is your reality. It is a daily reminder of what you are striving for and to help you stay in vibrational alignment with your goals.

All the goal setting in the world will not just simply make things happen, this alone is not 'magic'. However, if you combine your goal setting with inspired action, that there is real-life adult magic! Inspired action is coming up in the next chapter.

INSPIRED ACTION

> *Action without vision is only passing time,*
> *vision without action is merely daydreaming*
> *but vision with action can change the world.*

— NELSON MANDELA

What I came to learn from the many mistakes I made along the way in learning about the Law of Attraction, was that without INSPIRED action, it was all pointless. It was not magic; a board with pictures on it and happy thoughts would not make for dreams coming true, much as a little box with bits of paper with some words scribbled on them, is exactly that, just a little box filled with scrap paper. I started to believe I had been sold a lie, my life had not changed like the people telling me it would if I did all this shit they were telling me to do; putting stupid bloody pictures on my social media and announcing my public accountability. I have a few choice words for this now if you had not already guessed!

There is a secret ingredient required to activate this so-called magic! It is ACTION, well actually not just any old action, ten-star jumps, and patting on your head while you rub your tummy will not have you buying your own island next to Sir Richard Branson. INSPIRED ACTION. The kind of action, which is guided to you by your soul, not your ego. It feels responsive, not reactive to thought.

Inspired action comes from that place within you that you cannot physically see; it is your intuition, your higher self, your gut founded ideas. These are the places you find inspired action and you find it through a deeper connection to yourself. The quickest and easiest way to hearing your intuition is through meditation. The moments in the day where you are alone and the air around you is filled with silence. Be at one with yourself and the surroundings around you. Please do not beat the drum of repeating you don't have time, you don't have time, you don't have time. Chapter One should have helped you establish that you make the time for the things that you gain the most value from. Is finding a few moments in the day alone to fill with silence something you may gain value from? If change is what you want and a life that makes your heart sing is on the horizon, you need to take this seriously. Find the moments to listen for that idea, that thought that pops up, that feeling that you need to go and do something or call someone, that is inspired. It came from nowhere, it feels right and it does not always make sense at the time but consider this thought process as following the trail of breadcrumbs left by the Universe for you to find and follow that is responsive to your thought.

You will find in time that you do not need to actively ask your soul for these thoughts, as you progress along your spiritual pathway and become more aware of your spiritual self, you will develop a connection to yourself which is unshakable. It will become second nature to hear these thoughts and recognise them for what they are. Making decisions from this place of thought is easy and it feels good. These higher vibrations of energy/thought bring with it a feeling of ease and grace. The Law of Attraction needs not to make a huge deal of sense to you if you are just beginning to embrace it, however if you are living your life in flow with the Universe you are said to be following the path of least resistance. Taking note of the road markers and diversions along the way, it may not look like the most direct route, but it is the most efficient route for the vibration of thought which you are matched to. Or perhaps you could view it as the Universe sending you little guides to help you along the way, these guides come in the form of people, ideas, or opportunities. Anything that feels like it came along for a reason and helps you towards where you are heading. Coincidence? I think not. Experiences like this are called synchronicities. The Universe is always sending you more of what you are thinking the good the bad and the ugly. So be mindful of your thoughts.

Trusting yourself to hear inspired thoughts can be a challenge in the beginning, especially if you are guilty of being an over-thinker. You can drive yourself loopy thinking too much into a thought which popped into your mind. Take a breath and relax, this is not a deal-breaking situation. Remember that the Universe will only send you what you can handle at any one time. No decision or action is wrong as you discover its relevance to your life, you can re-adjust action whenever you feel fit. If you feel you made the wrong decision, change it.

Most people do not think like this, most people do not live spiritually in tune with themselves and therefore this way of thinking may seem indirect and evasive to them. It is certainly not a way of living that many of us will have experienced throughout our lives, so I can understand if this all feels a little much right now, just trust that it will open your life up to new and exciting opportunities. What do you have to lose by giving it a go?

Most of us will have been encouraged to think logically and practically throughout our lives. We usually make decisions from a place where information and facts are the foundations of any place of thought, it can feel very strange to change the way you think suddenly. What I suggest you do is just practice with it regularly, ask yourself little questions in your day and begin to tune into the answers as they are given you to, we generally choose not to hear them because sometimes it is an answer we do not want to hear. Start small with day to day stuff like:

Which outfit should I wear?

Where shall we go on the weekend?

Play around with what you hear, if you are guided to visit a certain place on the weekend ask yourself, "What will I learn there?" Are you going to see something that will amaze the children? Spend time during the visit to observe the surroundings be aware of the heart singing moments, watch the look of joy on the faces around you and really be mindful of the experience you have been guided to see; there is a reason everything happens. Absolutely everything that happens to you in life is a lesson of some sort and your job is to decipher the code and grow from each experience. Find the joy in everything as there is joy to be found all around you.

THE POWER IN A QUOTE

 One word can change someone's entire day.

— UNKNOWN

Quotes are a wonderful source of inspiration. They mesmerize with their ability to inspire in just a few short words and hold so much power over our perspective. I use quotes regularly to bring my thinking into check or to be recharged with inspiration. Picking a favourite would be impossible for me. I am inspired in different ways on different days and the words speak to me in the way I need to hear them. Sometimes I daydream about becoming the author of a well-known quote, you know much like Michele Obama and Oprah are shared online by Prince Ea frequently. Oh, to be shared by Prince Ea!!

I have arranged a collection of quotes which I find particularly powerful and that have stopped me in my tracks to ponder my thoughts over each one at different times. I hope this proves to be a source of inspiration for you and somewhere you can return to and be inspired on days where the ego's voice is turned up a little too loud.

You can silence negative thoughts incredibly quickly through a well-worded quote. As always feel free to join in the conversation online with The Mindset Mum on FB or Insta and share your favourites.

> *It is not your position, but your disposition which determines your happiness.*

— UNKNOWN

> *I found the paradox, that if I love until it hurts there is no hurt, only more love.*

— MOTHER THERESA

> *People will forget what you said, people will forget what you did, but people will never forget how you made them feel.*

— MAYA ANGELO

Be the change you wish to see in the world.

— GANDHI

Be kind and have courage.

— ANNE FRANK

Do not judge others until you have walked a mile in their shoes.

— AMERICAN PROVERB

We all have two lives, the second begins when you realise you only have one.

— CONFUCIUS

When the student is ready the teacher appears.

— BUDDHIST PROVERB

You are never given a wish without also being given the power to make it come true.

— RICHARD BACH

Do not let the behaviour of others destroy your inner peace.

— DALAI LAMA

Nothing in life has any meaning except the meaning we give it.

— TONY ROBBINS

A negative mind will never give you a positive life.

— ZIAD K ABDELNOUR

Success is not final. Failure is not fatal. It is the courage to continue that counts.

— WINSTON CHURCHILL

How wonderful is it that nobody needs to wait a single moment before starting to improve the world?

— ANNE FRANK

Sometimes it takes a good fall to know where you stand.

— HAYLEY WILLIAMS

When writing the story of your life, do not let anyone else hold the pen.

— HARLEY DAVIDSON

We are not human beings having a spiritual experience, we are spiritual beings having a human experience.

— PIERRE TEILHARD DE CHARDIN

Keep your face to the sun and the shadows will fall behind you.

— MAORI PROVERB

On the highest throne in the world, we still sit only on our own bottom.

— MICHEL DE MONTAIGNE

> *You are never too old to set another goal or to dream a new dream.*

— C. S. LEWIS

> *It is better to live one day as a lion than 1000 days as a sheep.*

— TIBETAN PROVERB

> *Those who wish to sing will always find a song.*

— SWEDISH PROVERB

> *Money is numbers and numbers never end. If it takes money to be happy, your search for happiness will never end.*

— BOB MARLEY

> *Stop worrying about what can go wrong and get excited about what can go right.*

— UNKNOWN

If you are going to laugh about it in five years, you may as well laugh about it now.

— ANONYMOUS

Worry does not empty tomorrow of its sorrow. It empties today of its strength.

— CORRIE TEN BOOM

Be kinder than necessary. Everyone you meet is facing some kind of problem.

— J. M. BARRIE

Yesterday is history, tomorrow is a mystery. Today is a gift that is why it's called the present.

— ELEANOR ROOSEVELT

Do or do not. There is no try.

— MASTER YODA

Walk where there is no path and leave your own trail.

— RALPH WALDO EMERSON

I never lose. I either win or learn.

— NELSON MANDELA

When you focus on problems you find more problems, when you focus on possibilities you will find more possibilities.

— ZIG ZIGLAR

The world as we created it is a process of our thinking. It cannot be changed without changing our thinking.

— ALBERT EINSTEIN

You are never wrong to do the right thing.

— MARK TWAIN

Do the best you can until you know better; then when you know better do better.

— MAYA ANGELO

Everyone knew it could not be done until a fool who did not know came along and did it.

— ALBERT EINSTEIN

Doubt kills more dreams than failure ever will.

— SUZY KASSEM

Trust the process.

— AMERICAN SPORTING SLOGAN

Who you become is infinitely more important than what you do or what you have.

— MATTHEW KELLY

We do not make mistakes, simply happy little accidents.

— BOB ROSS

Progress is impossible without change, and those who cannot change their minds cannot change anything.

— GEORGE BERNARD SHAW

We cannot solve our problems with the same thinking we used to create them.

— ALBERT EINSTEIN

Everyone thinks of changing the world, but no one thinks of changing himself.

— LEO TOLSTOY

When we are no longer able to change a situation, we are challenged to change ourselves.

— VIKTOR E FRANKL

I am no longer accepting the things I cannot change. I am changing the things I cannot accept.

— ANGELA DAVIS

Silence the outside world to hear the whispers of the Universe.

— CLAIRE MACGILLIVRAY

Do not be ashamed of your story, it will inspire others.

— UNKNOWN

The secret of change is to focus all your energy not on fighting the old, but on building the new.

— DAN MILLMAN

Change is never easy but always possible.

— BARACK OBAMA

We delight in the beauty of the butterfly but rarely admit the changes it has gone through to achieve that beauty.

— MAYA ANGELOU

LET'S CONNECT!

"Let's connect!"

It is such a modern phrase to say and the nineties kid in me wants to take the royal piss right out of it but I shall decline the impulse and ride the wave of modern ways.

All jokes aside I do enjoy making new connections with people of my 'sort' online. Sadly, I missed out with online dating; I met Trev through the old-fashioned way and find myself deeply intrigued by the stories of online dating from my friends who have the joy of embracing it. I reckon I would have had a lot of fun swiping my way to love! Although I am very grateful for my conventional meeting with Trev all those years ago and we have made 3 very beautiful children together.

There are several ways you can connect with me online. The place I tend to hang out most is in my Facebook Group:

@ TheMindsetMum
www.facebook.com/groups/themindsetmum

I am trying (I would be lying if I said my hardest) to get my head into Insta and all the Insta perfect shit on there, I am not a natural Instagrammer, my day to day can be very messy and if you see a post from me on there you can be assured it has been a mish to get it taken and tagged, oh the bloody hashtags. I keep hearing my audience are there so get my ass in the game. Like I said, I am trying and you will find me on Insta using the handle the_mindset_mum come and check out my grid!

For all the downloads I have mentioned in the book, scrap that, not plural just the one download. One meditation is all you're getting! You can find that on my website www.themindsetmum.com (I will add more freebies as the inspiration drives me to).

I would love to hear how this book has helped you so please do share your stories with me. Please also leave a review on Amazon or Goodreads after you finish the book. I have promised myself to only read the good ones, so if it is a stinker I will never know. Well I dare say I will get wind of it but bear in mind this is my first book so be kind. Remember the chapter on returning to Love? Let those words channel their way to you.

I also promised you I would share the connections for my spiritual mentors Olivia and Raf Ocana. You can find them on Facebook and Insta in '5th Dimension Earth'. They have also written two books and they are available on Amazon. The first one is called '25 Messages From Heaven' and the second book is called 'Believe'. I have read both books and refer to them regularly. Believe is my spiritual bible. The insights that are shared within those pages are absolutely incredible and have never been written about previously. If you are wanting to progress further along your spiritual pathway I can strongly recommend any and all teachings from Olivia and Raf.

ACKNOWLEDGEMENTS

Many minds have contributed to the creation of this book and it has left me in awe of the generosity from those of whom helped me pull this out of the proverbial bag. My appreciation and gratitude are in abundance towards you and my deepest thanks to each and every one of you.

 Bonnie not only are you my oldest and dearest friend you are also a bombshell with words, and you have seriously kept my 'over comma using' ass in check. You were the first person to give me the belief that I could do this [book] long before I ever believed it myself and without your unwavering encouragement this would not have become the book it has today. Thank you.

Helen Poole my illustrator, cover designer, book formatter and all-round superhero! You are a fountain of book knowledge and you have been invaluable to me along this journey. We were pulled together with Universal force and continue to share synchronicities which always make my heart sing. You have created the physical manifestation of my thoughts in the book cover, thank you for bringing my ideas to life. You have been a joy to work with.

Thank you to all my Beta readers. Zara, Sally, Mhiz, and Sian your feedback has been invaluable and without it I would have been walking down the street with the author's equivalent of toilet roll stuck to my shoe! You pointed things out to me that I was blind to as the writer, thank you for volunteering your time to me.

To Trev and the children, what can I say besides thank you from the bottom of my heart for not ever asking me why it is taking me so long to write my book? You have supported me without question and backed off when you felt it was right to give me room to be creative. Thank you for trusting the process.

And finally, a huge thanks to you the reader for picking this book over the millions to choose from and parting with your hard-earned bucks to purchase it. I hope that somewhere within these pages you have found a shared experience or a relatable feeling and with that you have also found a way of seeing the lighter side to it and an awareness of not being alone in your strive for balance. Be like the butterfly and emerge from this book with your wings ready to flutter.

Thank you for reading.